AMERICAN CITIES CHRONOLOGY SERIES

MILWAUKEE
A CHRONOLOGICAL & DOCUMENTARY HISTORY

1673-1977

Compiled and Edited by
GEORGE J. LANKEVICH

Series Editor
HOWARD B. FURER

1977
OCEANA PUBLICATIONS, INC.
Dobbs Ferry, New York

For George and Christine

Library of Congress Cataloging in Publication Data

Lankevich, George J., 1939-

Milwaukee: a chronological & documentary history,
   1673-1977.

   (American cities chronology series)
   Bibliography: p.
   Includes index.
   SUMMARY: A chronology of events in the history
of Milwaukee from 1673 to 1977 accompanied by
pertinent documents.
      1. Milwaukee — History — Chronology. 2. Milwaukee —
History — Sources. [1. Milwaukee — History] I. Title
F589.M657M54   977.5'95   77-8947
ISBN 0-379-00620-0

Manufactured in the United States of America

TABLE OF CONTENTS

EDITOR'S FOREWORD

The city of Milwaukee is best described as a "small-
town metropolis." Although it is the twelfth largest
American city and center of the nineteenth largest metropolitan district in the nation, Milwaukee's attitudes
are dominated by the old fashioned virtues of thrift,
hard work, self-sufficiency, and family living. Milwaukee has long been, and remains now, a city of historical contrasts. Once America's "most foreign" city, it
is today one of the most homogeneous. Yet as its foreign elements became acculturated, they maintained their
ethnic traditions and created a city that blended the
Old with the New World. Milwaukee once possessed the
most lurid reputation in the Midwest, yet today it is a
highly moral community where "if a man walks into a bar
with a girl young enough to be his daughter, she probably is." In Milwaukee, modern industry coexists with a
tradition of skilled craftsmanship and the resultant
combination has made the city America's third largest metropolitan exporter of machinery; it leads the world in
producing items as diverse as diesel engines and beer.
And although the city's reputation has long centered on
its breweries, only once in its history (and that almost
ninety years ago) has brewing been its most important
industry. Today only two percent of Milwaukee's labor
is devoted to the industry that made it famous throughout
the world, and the city is far more accurately labeled
"America's Workshop." The contrasts go on and on. The
Milwaukee area is a veritable paradise for the individual
sportsman, yet the city carries on a passionate love
affair with its professional athletic teams. Far removed from the ocean, the city has become an international trader of note because of the opening of the St. Laurence Seaway. In domestic politics the city is staunchly
Democratic, yet its present mayor calls it conservative;
historically it long elected Socialists to high office. Milwaukee's black and white communities are deeply
divided, yet all its citizens resent the "iron ring" of
bedroom suburbs that surround them. Few American cities
are able to match Milwaukee's glorious variety. Citizens
of the "Cream City of the Lakes," whether considered
small town Americans or struggling urbanites, are heirs
to a tradition of accomplishment and change that augurs
well for the future of their city.

George J. Lankevich
Bronx Community College
of the City University
of New York

FRONTIER VILLAGE
1673-1845

1673-1674   Father Jacques Marquette, guided by Louis
             Joliet, skirts the shoreline of Milwaukee
             Bay. The name probably stems from the Pot-
             towatomie language, the word "Mahn-ah-wauk"
             meaning a gathering place or council ground
             by the water.

1679   Led by Father Zenobius Membré, some of La-
             Salle's exploratory expedition probably halt
             at Milwaukee; the site of "Melleoiki" is
             listed in French missionary records. Three
             rivers, the Milwaukee, the Menomonee, the
             Kinnickinnic, meet in Milwaukee Bay, and the
             site becomes a fur trading center.

1699   October 7. Father Jean Buisson de St. Cosme
             visits the Milwaukee area, claiming lands
             which remain under French control until
             1763.

1776   With the outbreak of revolution, the tribes
             of the Milwaukee area prove more favorable to
             the American cause than any other Midwestern
             tribes.

1779   November. The British commander at Michill-
             imackinac condemns the "horrid set of re-
             fractory Indians" at Milwaukee as renegades.
             H.M.S. Felicity, a sloop, stops at Milwaukee
             in November to impress the Indians with Bri-
             tish power.

1784   March 1. Virginia cedes all her claims over
             Northwest lands to the United States.

1795   August 20. Jacques Vieau settles south of
             the Menomonee River and establishes a North-
             west Co. Trading Post. Aided by Jean Bap-
             tiste Mirandeau, Vieau sends regular ship-
             ments of furs to Detroit and Mackinac.

1800   Antoine le Claire organizes a fur station
             north of the Milwaukee River.

1803   Captain Thomas Anderson trades with Milwaukee
             and finds a settlement of some 300, including
             traders, Indians, and even a blacksmith.

1812-1815   During the second war with Britain, when
             most Wisconsin tribes favored the English,

the Milwaukee area Indians led by Old Flour
of the Menominee, maintain neutrality.

1817   A British census reported 1000 persons in the
            Milwaukee area, a land of marsh, tamarack
            swamp, and extensive stands of timber.

1818   April 18. By order of General Lewis Cass
            all military posts in the Milwaukee area are
            attached to the Chicago Indian Agency.

            September 14. Solomon Juneau arrives in
            Milwaukee and establishes an American Fur
            Company post east of the Milwaukee River.
            Quebec-born Juneau soon becomes the first
            citizen of the settlement, tames renegade
            Indians with his fists, and marries Jacques
            Vieau's daughter, Josette.

1824   Juneau constructs the first frame building in
            Milwaukee.

1830   The U. S. Census reports 3,245 residents in
            all of Wisconsin. John Farmer publishes a
            map of the Northwest that shows "Milwalky"
            Bay.

1831   February 8. A treaty is signed with the Me-
            nominee Indians that cedes to the United
            States all lands north and east of the Mil-
            waukee River.

            June 15. Solomon Juneau becomes a natural-
            ized citizen of the United States.

            August 31. Land in the Milwaukee area is
            first offered for sale in Green Bay.

1832   The Black Hawk War erupts in Illinois and
            the Milwaukee area becomes a haven for
            friendly Indians.

1833   July-August. Morgan L. Martin, a Green Bay
            speculator, visits Milwaukee and draws a
            map showing swamps, high bluffs, and only
            three houses. His map convinces Secretary
            of War Lewis Cass to order a land survey.

            September 26. The Pottawatomie Indians cede
            to the United States all lands they claim
            south and west of the Milwaukee River.

            October. Martin and Juneau conclude a gen-

tlemen's agreement, a partnership dividing
property rights and looking toward the development of a townsite.

November 18. Four additional white settlers
arrive and spend the winter with Juneau. An
epidemic of smallpox during the winter kills
many Indians and convinces Jacques Vieau
that the site has no future.

1834   March 20. George Walker of Virginia arrives
in Milwaukee and establishes himself on the
point of land south of the harbor entrance.

May. Byron Kilbourn arrives and settles on
the west side of the Milwaukee River, an area
closer to the trade of the hinterland.

Summer. William S. Trowbridge carries out
the first lot survey in Milwaukee. The
settlers request $15,000 from Congress for
harbor development.

September 6. Milwaukee County is created by
the Michigan legislature.

December. President Andrew Jackson appoints
Juneau Milwaukee's first postmaster -- a
position he holds until 1843.

1835   March 17. The Michigan legislature creates
the town of Milwaukee.

April 9. Doctor Enoch Chase, Milwaukee's
first physician, arrives. Methodist services are held in his home in early May.

June 17. The Michigan is the first steamship to enter Milwaukee harbor, but because
of obstructions its passengers are ferried
ashore. Horace Chase establishes a ferry
at the mouth of the Milwaukee River.

July. The Reverend A. L. Barber holds the
first Presbyterian services in Milwaukee.
The first hotel and tavern open.

August 1. The Green Bay land office begins
sale of land in the Milwaukee area. The
Juneau-Morgan partnership purchases lands on
the east side of the river, while Kilbourn
purchases lands to the west. Both groups are
selling homesites to settlers and competing

for their support.

August 25. Milwaukee County is created though
reduced in size by the Michigan legislature.

August. Father J. Bonduel offers Milwaukee's
first Catholic Mass in the home of Solomon
Juneau.

August-September. Nelson Olin produces bricks
in his kiln. They emerge with a distinctive
cream color that will make Milwaukee "The
Cream City of the Lakes." Olin produces
10,000 bricks in September alone and his kiln
is soon joined by one operated by William
Sivyer, By the fall the site has two saw-
mills, a warehouse, three stores, and at
least twenty-five houses.

September 8. Juneau's land deeds are recorded,

September 17. The first town election is
held, with all settlers entitled to vote.
Thirty-nine voters, among them a black, e-
lect twenty-four officials. George Walker
is elected first town supervisor.

October 8. Kilbourn's land deeds are recorded,

October 10. Miss Milwaukee Smith is the
first white child to be born in Milwaukee.

December 12. A public meeting petitions
Congress for preemption laws and for an appropriation to build a canal or a railroad
west to the Rock River.

December 19. A second citizens meeting asks
Congress to appropriate money for a lighthouse and for harbor development. Congress
responds by approving $400 during 1836.

1836   January-August. A period of intense land
speculation begins, as the two sides of the
river, Juneautown and Kilbourntown, compete
to become the heart of the town.

March. Weekly stage operation to Chicago begins; this aids Kilbourntown because the Chicago road bypasses the east side of the river.

April 4. The first election of county officials is held in Juneau's home, and all
participants then adjourn to a tavern.

May 4. Charles Sivyer, Milwaukee's first
white boy, is born.

June 13. Grading begins on East Water
Street in Juneautown. Juneau contributes
$6,000 to finance the project whose incep-
tion is celebrated by the drinking of thirty
baskets of champagne -- Milwaukee is still
beerless. Not to be outdone, Kilbourne
builds a bridge across the Menomonee River
to divert all road traffic to his settlement.

Summer. Competition between the two villages
intensifies. Juneau and Martin donate land
and money to construct a courthouse and a
jail on the east side. Kilbourn spends
$25,000 to improve facilities on the west
side of the Milwaukee.

July 4. Wisconsin becomes a separate territory -- one that includes parts of Iowa,
Minnesota, and both Dakotas.

July 14. The Milwaukee Advertiser, the third
newspaper in Wisconsin, begins to publish in
Kilbourntown. Increase Lapham, a budding
scientist, arrives and candidly reports that
most homes are located in Juneautown.

September. Juneau organizes the Milwaukee
Steamboat Company.

September 22, Kilbourn chairs a meeting
that calls for a railroad to the Mississippi,
and a Committee of Fifteen (including Juneau)
is appointed to investigate the proposal.

October 25. The first territorial legislature
convenes in Belmont, Iowa.

November. Two whites kill an Indian, the
first murder in what will become America's
safest city.

December. The Wisconsin legislature charters
the Bank of Milwaukee. Financial panic ruins
its business and the charter is repealed
within three years.

A school is conducted by Edward West this
winter, but there will be no free public
school until the city is incorporated.

The population of the Milwaukee area is es-
timated to be 1200.

1837   January 17. Juneau's grant of courthouse
park lands to the east side is recorded.

February 27. Both Juneau and Kilbourn petition the territory for town incorporation.
Juneau is elected President of the Village
of Milwaukee while Kilbourn continues to dominate the west side.

March 13. Milwaukee County residents create
a claim organization whose purpose is to
protest the pre-emption rights of original
settlers versus speculators.

April. Presbyterians organize the first
church in Milwaukee, although a building
is not constructed until 1840.

June 27. The Milwaukee Sentinel begins to
publish on the east side. Other community
developments include formation of the first
fire company by Benjamin Edgerton, the first
medical society by Dr. Thomas Noyes, the
first county agricultural society by Increase Lapham, and the first temperance society. The U. S. District Court begins to
sit.

July 27. Milwaukee launches its first ship,
the 90-ton schooner Juneau, built by George
Barber. Not to be outdone, Kilbourn finances
the first steamship, The Badger, which brings
passengers from the harbor only to the west
side.

Juneau and Martin open the Milwaukee House
Hotel.

Fall. Father Patrick Kelly arrives in Milwaukee, and will hold Catholic services in
the courthouse for the next two years.

December 5. John O'Rourke, editor of the
Sentinel, dies and is succeeded by Harrison
Reed.

1838   January 5. The Milwaukee and Rock River Canal Co., a Kilbourn project, is incorporated by the Wisconsin Legislature. It plans a canal to the Mississippi, but only a mile of that canal, and a dam, ever will be completed.

March. The election for three county commissioners is won by Kilbourn's West Siders.

April. An Episcopal diocese is created in Milwaukee.

June 18. Congress authorizes the cession of odd-numbered sections along the Rock River Canal to the company.

July 4. Ground is broken for the Rock River Canal.

A 50-foot lighthouse is completed at the foot of Water Street on the east side.

September 18. The Sentinel calls for a railroad and derides the canal project.

December. A census conducted by H. W. Olin confirms that depression has reduced Milwaukee's population to 700.

1839   January 10. Lucius I. Barber organizes the Milwaukee Lyceum.

January 21. The second territorial legislature convenes in Madison with Barber as speaker, and another Milwaukeean, Horatio Wells, as territorial attorney general.

February 16-March 19. The first government land sales in the Milwaukee District are held. The Claims Organization prevents speculation, and most lands are purchased by the pioneers.

March 11. The Town of Milwaukee is incorporated as the legislature merges the east and west side villages.

May 1. The first election in the new town is held. Each ward elects five trustees; Juneau is named president of the consolidated council.

May 7. The legislature incorporates the Wis-

consin Marine and Fire Insurance Co., a bank
in all but name, which under the direction
of Alexander Mitchell will dominate Milwaukee's development for forty years. Its modern heir is the Marine National Exchange
Bank.

May. St. Peters, the first Catholic Church
in Milwaukee, opens.

Summer. Irishmen from Fall River, Massachu-
setts, and German immigrants arrive in
large numbers.

September 1. Constructed with a congressional grant of $10,000, a seventy-nine mile
road to Madison is opened.

James Doty defeats Kilbourn and is elected
Milwaukee's delegate to the territorial legislature.

December 6. The "Great Harbor" Meeting demands federal funds to develop the Milwaukee
Harbor. Land sales in 1839 total $738,522.

1840   January 11. The Wisconsin Legislature orders
all male residents of Milwaukee to serve two
days of street repair annually.

February 14. The volunteer Neptune Fire Company is organized by George Dousman.

April. Three Welshmen found Milwaukee's
first brewery (ale).

The east side launches its first steamer,
the C.C. Trowbridge.

A drawbridge constructed by the county opens
at Chestnut and Division streets. Competition between the wards is so intense that
the streets "break joints" at the river, and
even today Milwaukee's streets do not run
smoothly into each other when they cross
the river.

April 30. The Town of Wauwautoosa is incorporated.

May. H. M. Hubbard is elected president of
the Consolidated Village of Milwaukee.

June. The first brew made in Milwaukee is produced by the three Welshmen. Milwaukee today is the world's leading beer city both in consumption and production.

December. Milwaukee's population is 1,712; in the 1840's its growth outpaces Chicago's.

1841 January 1. Twelve thousand Whigs converge on Milwaukee to celebrate the election of President William H. Harrison. However, their roasted ox is stolen by Kilbourntown Democrats.

March 27. Publisher D. Richards sells the Milwaukee *Advertiser*, which becomes the *Courier* under James Noonan.

April. A new board of town commissioners is elected.

Herman Reuthlisberger opens Milwaukee's first lager brewery.

May. J. H. Rogers is elected town president.

May 20. The first Congregational Bethel Church, which becomes Plymouth Church (August, 1850), is formed: John Miter is the first pastor

July 8. The *Illinois* carries 4,000 bushels of wheat to Canada. This is the first major export of grain from Milwaukee, which had compiled a $6,000,000 trade deficit from 1835-41.

July 9. Juneau's steamship *Milwaukee* runs aground in the river and is ultimately lost.

August. The Milwaukee *Journal* (Elisha Starr, editor) first appears.

October. James Doty is elected territorial governor.

1842 February 17. Increase Lapham and F. Randall issue a report on lake commerce; 118 persons died and eighty-nine ships were lost between 1834 and 1841. They ask federal money for harbor development. Merchant Horatio Stevens erects Milwaukee's first pier at Huron Street.

April. All improvements are consolidated
under a three man board of street commissioners and by July, gravel sidewalks service
the entire town. Charles Dewey constructs
the first block of brick stores and the
Milwaukee and Rock River completes a short
canal parallel to the Milwaukee River.

Summer. Three Milwaukee men help a fugitive
slave, Caroline Quarles, escape to Canada.

September 27. Lyman and Powell's Detroit
and Chicago Co. performs the first plays in
Milwaukee, The Merchant of Venice and William
Tell.

November. Philetus Hale, proprietor of Milwaukee's only bookstore, opens a circulating
library.

December 30. The Mechanic's Protective Association is organized.

December 31. Milwaukee's population has
soared to 2,700. The town has 800 buildings,
twelve inns and fifty stores.

1843   January. Edward D. Holton organizes and becomes president of the Beethoven Society.

March 3. Congress allots $30,000 for harbor
development. The resident army engineer in
Milwaukee ultimately decides to improve the
natural outlet of the Milwaukee River rather
than construct a "straight cut" through sand
dunes to Lake Michigan.

March 23. Milwaukee's German population,
led by Franz Huebschmann, celebrates the
congressional appropriation with a Harbor
Festival.

Spring-Fall. Milwaukee suffers an extended
smallpox epidemic.

April. A German string quartet performs
Milwaukee's first concert.

A floating bridge at Spring Street is completed, replacing the ferry between the east
and west wards.

May. E. D. Holton is elected sheriff, and

Lindsay Ward president of the Consolidated Town.

June 1. A 1200-foot pier at the mouth of the river is completed. When the lake steamer <u>Cleveland</u> disembarks passengers directly into town trade prospects brighten.

June 17. After an attempt to construct a "Straight cut" without army aid has failed, the West Siders authorize construction of a pier at the site of the proposed cut. The project fails, and the U. S. engineers complete improvements at the river's mouth.

July 5. Lodge #22 of the Masonic Order is organized.

July 20. A meeting is held protesting Juneau's removal as postmaster and his replacement by James Noonan.

August. C. C. Scholes founds the <u>Milwaukee Democrat</u>.

November 28. Milwaukee is created a diocese of the Roman Catholic Church.

December. Milwaukee completes its most prosperous trading year: 2,000,000 lbs. of lead have been exported along with grain stores. A local grist mill is in operation. Thousands of immigrants have completed the four and a half day trip from Buffalo, and the permanent population of the town has passed 3,000.

1844   January 22. The territorial legislature decides that all free white males over twenty-one years of age and residents in Wisconsin for three months, can vote in the statehood referendum.

March 19. John M. Henni is consecrated the first Catholic Bishop of Milwaukee.

April. Juneau declares bankruptcy.

Milwaukee votes $15,000 to develop a "straight cut" and Congress approves an additional $20,000 for harbor improvements.

Jacob Best opens a brewery that ultimately

becomes Pabst Beer Company.

May 5. Bishop Henni conducts his first services in Milwaukee partly in the German
language.

July 19. A German fire company is organized.

August 16. A free float bridge from Walker's
Point is opened.

August 21. The Milwaukee City Guards are
organized.

September 7. The weekly Wiskonsin-Banner,
a German paper, is first published. The
Milwaukee Democrat moves to Waukeska, where
it becomes the American Freeman.

A Wisconsin referendum decides against or-
ganizing a state government.

September 30. John Anderson opens Milwaukee's first flour mill; this same month
John Plankinton opens a leather shop and a
pork packing house.

December 9. The Daily Sentinel (C. L. Mac-
Arthur, editor) first appears.

December 20. A mass meeting appoints a
committee to draft a city charter, but its
proposals fail because of opposition to any
suffrage limitations.

1845   January 19. Milwaukee instructs its representatives to the territorial legislature
to oppose all charter legislation.

January 23. The Sentinel establishes a
public reading room.

A militia company, the Washington Guards,
is organized.

February 12. Walker's Point becomes Milwaukee's South Ward.

February 22. Best & Co. sells its first lager beer.

April 6-7. A great fire consumes two blocks
of stores, destroying $90,000 worth of pro-

perty.

May 3. A schooner crash into the Spring
Street Bridge precipitates the "Bridge War"
between the East and West wards.

May 7. The three wards meet in common council for the first time after the west-siders
destroy the Chestnut Street Bridge.

May 8. With only one west sider attending
the council meeting, Kilbourn supporter
E. D. Holton is voted out as president and
is replaced by L. W. Weeks.

May 15. Town trustees vote to repair the
Chestnut Street Bridge and to discontinue
the Oneida Bridge.

May 19. West siders, inspired by Kilbourn,
wreck the Spring Street Bridge.

May 28. East siders destroy the Menomonee
River Bridge and threaten destruction of the
Rock River Dam.

June 2. A special council committee recommends that three permanent bridges be constructed at Milwaukee, none to impede river
traffic.

June 3. The _Sentinel_ employs newsboys for
the first time to hawk the papers that pro-
claim settlement of the War.

Summer. Asa Whitney leads a survey team that
discovers good rail routes to the Mississippi.

September 29. Rufus King becomes owner and
editor of the Milwaukee _Sentinel_.

November 2. A schooner again crashes into
the Spring Street Bridge but renewed war
does not occur.

November 18. Daily mail service to Chicago
is established.

November. Milwaukee ships its first packaged
beef and pork products. The port also exports 7,550 barrels of excellent flour during
this year.

December 12. Rufus King leads demands for
a school system -- thirteen schools, four of
which are public, exist in Milwaukee, but
fewer than a third of potential students
attend any school.

December 20. The council creates the Milwaukee Fire Department.

CITY IN THE WILDERNESS
1846-1869

1846   January 5. Milwaukee votes on a charter
proposed by D. A. J. Upham; the combined
votes of the west and south wards carry the
charter to victory.

January 31. The City of Milwaukee is incorporated. The charter grants to each of five
wards great autonomy in financial matters,
limits the power of the mayor, and organizes
Waukeska into an independent county.

February 3. Wisconsin authorizes a Milwaukee
board of school commissioners and orders that
the cost of future bridges be allotted evenly
among all five wards.

March. Michael Skupniewicz, Milwaukee's first
Polish immigrant, arrives.

April 7. Milwaukee's first charter election
is held. Solomon Juneau is elected mayor
of a city of 7.3 square miles, "five villages slightly connected together."

April 10. The village trustees turn over
city management to the new mayor and a fifteen-man common council.

April 14. Three school commissioners from
each ward meet and elect Rufus King president of the school board. By the end of the
year they organize a system of six public
schools serving 700 pupils.

April. St. Mary's Church, for German Roman
Catholics, sets its cornerstone.

August 27. G. P. Hewitt is named chief of
the fire department.

September. The first board of health (Juneau and five doctors) is established to deal with an outbreak of smallpox.

Milwaukee elects twelve delegates to the Wisconsin Constitutional Convention.

October. Increase Lapham donates thirteen acres to establish a public high school, but the school board fails to accept the land.

December. A police nightwatch, a captain with a watchman in each ward, is established.

Milwaukee wheat exports rise to 213,448 bushels during 1846. City population spurts to 9,655.

1847   February 4. The Grand Avenue Congregational Church is founded.

February 10. Julius McCabe publishes the first city directory.

February 11. The legislature incorporates the Milwaukee and Waukesha Railroad.

March. Reappearance of a smallpox epidemic leads the council to call for the vaccination of all citizens.

April. The charter is amended to make the offices of treasurer, attorney and marshal elective. The council moves to a "City Hall" over a stable, where new Mayor Horatio N. Wells is inaugurated.

May. The Reliance Iron Works go into operation.

June. St. John's Episcopal Church, designed by Victor Schulte, opens.

June. The _Daily Wisconsin_ begins to publish.

Summer. The Milwaukee and Watertown Plank Road (toll) opens.

August 6. Enlistments begin for Mexican War volunteers.

September 11. Rosh Hashanah services, the first in Milwaukee and in Wisconsin, are held in the home of Henry Newhouse.

October 30. The Milwaukee Benevolent Society
for pauper relief is organized by Mrs. George
Hewitt.

December 8. The Young Men's Association,
founded by Rufus King, is organized to
bring lecturers to Milwaukee and to collect
volumes for a circulating library.

December 11. Milwaukee's City Medical Association is formed.

December 15. Wisconsin, having once rejected
a proposed constitution, convenes its Second
Constitutional Convention.

1848   January 17. Milwaukee receives its first
telegraph message over the lines of Ezra
Cornell's Erie and Michigan Telegraph Company.

March 13. Wisconsin votes to accept the
proposed state constitution, 16,799-6,384;
Milwaukee favors it 1,503-147.

April 12. Byron Kilborn is elected Mayor,
defeating Rufus King. His inaugural speech
stresses the advantages of railroad development; Kilbourn will be president of the first
railroad out of Milwaukee.

April 17. Milwaukee celebrates the outbreak
of revolutions in France, Germany, and Aus-
tria.

May. The American Freeman moves back to
Milwaukee where it becomes the Wisconsin
Free Democrat under the editorship of Sher-
man Booth.

May 29. Wisconsin is admitted to the Union
as the thirtieth state.

July. St. John's Infirmary opens. It is
the predecessor of St. Mary's Hospital.

September. The Milwaukee Female Seminary,
predecessor of Milwaukee College, opens under the direction of Lucy Parsons.

A month-long strike by the Ship's Carpenters

Association wins a ten-hour day from the
George Barber Yards.

November 29. John Rice opens Milwaukee's
first theater, presenting As You Like It.

December. Milwaukee boasts four flour mills
turning out 800 barrels daily. Its first
paper mill has been opened by the Ludington
and Garland Company.

1849   The Milwaukee Board of Trade is organized;
E. D. Holton is elected president of its
thirty-seven members.

George Walker secures firm title to his
south ward lands.

April. Democrat D. A. J. Upham defeats B. H.
Edgerton, the Peoples Candidate, and is elected mayor. He is a railroad zealot and begins the questionable practice of using the
city's credit to back loans to railroads.

July 19. The council, led by Upham, votes
a one per cent real estate tax to finance a
$100,000 purchase of Kilbourn's railroad
stock.

July-August. Cholera strikes the city; at
least 209 persons died in 1849, 104 during
these two months alone.

September. William Ashman builds the first
piano made in Milwaukee.

Increase Lapham demonstrates the existence
of a lunar tide in Lake Michigan.

December 8. A German amateur theater society
is organized. The German community is divided, however, between the liberal "48ers",
the "Greens" who read the Banner, and the
conservative Catholic "Grey's" who read der
Seebote.

December. Milwaukee's thirty-nine factories
produce $1,700,000 in goods, but the city
prospers largely on the basis of its wheat
and livestock trade.

1850   January. Morris Schoeffler's Banner becomes
the first German daily newspaper.

February 11. The Milwaukee and Waukesha becomes the Milwaukee and Mississippi Railroad. Its first track is put down in September.

March 4. A mob of 200-300 men destroys the
home of State Senator John B. Smith who had
won legislative approval of a tax of one
dollar per gallon of whisky and one dollar
per barrel (thirty-one gallons) of beer. The
economic sanction laid on the liquor trade
makes brewing an important industry.

April. Mayor Upham, a prohibitionist in
1849, is reelected with German support as
an opponent of any temperance legislation.

May 1. Hans Balatka organizes the Milwaukee
Musical Society.

May 25. The Musical Society gives its first
public concert.

July 15. The city's second Board of Health
is named to deal with a renewed cholera
outbreak -- c. 300 die before the empidemic
is contained.

September. Eighty-five of 150 Swedish immigrants die of typhus en route from Buffalo
to Milwaukee.

September 12. Milwaukee's first locomotive
arrives on the schooner _Abiah_ and is landed
by September 25 -- the railroad consists,
however, of only half a mile of track.

December. Population reaches 20,061 (sixty-
four per cent foreign born) with fully a
third of the total from Germany. Milwaukee
has grown over 1,000 per cent in a decade
and only thirteen per cent of city residents
are Wisconsin born.

1851   February 15. Young's Block of stores burns
to the ground.

February 21. The Milwaukee and Fond du Lac
Railroad is incorporated.

February 25. The first train runs over the
Milwaukee and Mississippi line to Waukesha.
However, Byron Kilbourn, the prime mover of

the scheme, is removed from the presidency.

March 1. A charter of incorporation is
granted to the Female Normal Institute and
High School.

March. The Wisconsin Legislature approves a
new charter for Milwaukee.

April 6. Milwaukee undergoes the "Leahy
Riot" as a mob of Catholics prevent an ex-
communicated priest from speaking. Edward
Leahy gives his talk, under police guard,
on April 8. The city votes $150 to repair
damage done to the Methodist Church.

May 6. The municipal debt reaches $400,000,
$234,000 of which is in credits extended to
railroads. In the city election the voters
reject a check on spending, yet elect George
Walker mayor, whose platform promises reduced city expenditures.

July 2. The Milwaukee Musical Society presents the first of three performances of
Haydn's <u>Creation</u>。

August. A popularly elected convention,
chaired by Hans Crocker, drafts a new city
charter.

August 21. A school census reports that
5,914 children attend the public schools
(1,668 Americans, 1,286 Irish, c. 400 others
and 2,577 Germans). The German children have
the option of studying their language in
public schools if they pay an extra fee. A
German English Academy (Schulverein) run by
Peter Engleman offers European style private
education.

November 4. The Wisconsin electorate approves
Prohibition (27,519-24,109).

December. The brewery of Valentine Blatz,
now merged with that of John Braun, reports
annual production of 150 barrels of its special beer.

1852   January 12. The Milwaukee Gas Light Co. is
created by John Lockwood.

February 15. Young's Hall burns down, depriving Milwaukee of a theater and the Musical Society of a home.

February 20. The voters approve the new charter by a vote of two to one. City boundaries are enlarged, while independence of the eight wards is reduced. Aldermen will serve as street commissioners.

March. Hans Crocker is elected mayor.

March 7. The Spring Street floating bridge collapses under a wagon of grain.

March 8. The Young Men's Public Library is incorporated.

April 2. The LaCrosse and Milwaukee Railroad is incorporated. Walton and Co. engineer James Waters constructs Milwaukee's first locomotive in the Menomonee River yards.

May. The German community holds Milwaukee's first May Fest.

August 19. The Milwaukee and Praire du Chien Railroad opens the first passenger terminal in Wisconsin.

November 23. Milwaukee is lit by gas lights for the first time-- seven miles of pipe are in operation by 1857. Improvements and political corruption force large tax increases each year to 1858.

December. Milwaukee breweries report the export of 645 barrels of beer during 1852.

1853   January 5. A bank charter is issued to the Wisconsin Marine and Fire Insurance Co.

January 23. John Rice's Theater burns down and he relocates in Chicago.

February 18. George Walker is reelected mayor on the People's ticket. The charter is further amended to make the offices of comptroller and city attorney elective. Railroad commissioners are to be named from each ward of the city.

April 8. The first German opera in the Mid-

west, <u>Zar und Zimmerman</u>, is produced by
the Music Society. Fourteen operas are per-
formed in Milwaukee from 1853-1860.

May 1. The Wisconsin State Bank opens.

May 2. The Farmers and Millers Bank opens.

May 17. Milwaukee voters approve 1,597-309
a city bond issue supporting the Green Bay,
Milwaukee and Chicago Railroad.

June 17. By a vote of 746-16 the voters approve bonds for the Milwaukee and Fond du
Lac Railroad.

June 23. City bonds for the LaCrosse and
Milwaukee Railroad are authorized, 1,300-16.

June 27. The Milwaukee, Fond du Lac and
Green Bay Railroad merges with the Milwaukee
and Fond du Lac Railroad.

July 11. Railway workers on the LaCrosse
and Milwaukee riot to obtain their back pay.

July 18. The Turnverein Society, an athletic
group for Germans, is organized by August
Willich.

July 31. The Cathedral of St. John is consecrated.

1853-57. Milwaukee finances a $900,000
street improvement project, cobblestone pav-
ing and sidewalks. These expenditures, in
combination with the credit expanded to railroads, nearly bankrupt the city.

1854   January 5. Demolition of the float bridge at
Wisconsin Avenue begins. Before the end of
the year, the first swing bridge across the
Milwaukee River will be in operation at this
site.

February. A public meeting led by King,
Kilbourn and Holton protests the Kansas-Neb-
raska Act.

March 7. A riot between Irish and German
voters mars the primary election.

March 11. A mob of Abolitionists from Ra-

cine, abetted by Milwaukee supporters and
inspired by Sherman Booth's oratory, frees
a captured fugitive slave (Joshua Glover)
from the Milwaukee jail and sends him to
freedom in Canada.

March 18. Byron Kilbourn defeats Walker and
becomes Milwaukee's mayor. The voters approve 50,000 dollars in bonds to finance a
"straight cut" to Lake Michigan, and work on
the project is begun by the army engineers.

April 1. The Milwaukee and Watertown Railroad is incorporated.

May 23. Rail connection with Madison is
achieved by the Milwaukee and Mississippi
Railroad.

June 8. A fierce lake storm beaches many
ships.

June 19. The Milwaukee City Guards are reorganized.

July 6. Milwaukee voters authorize additional bonds for the Milwaukee and Mississippi
Railroad by a vote of 529-23.

August 24. A $400,000 fire destroys the Uni-
ted States Hotel, the Mitchell Block stores,
and some thirty other buildings of downtown
Milwaukee.

1855   February 21. The Wisconsin legislature approves Milwaukee's annexation of 2.5 square
miles of adjoining lands.

March 6. Mayor Kilbourn closes the saloons
for election day, but "after four o'clock
p.m. you can let her go." In the election,
James B. Cross defeats Comptroller Cicero
Comstock and becomes mayor. Cross opposes
the "Tax eating" council led by Jackson
Hadley but is unable to prevent passage of
further subsidies to railroads.

March 14. The first Y.M.C.A. meeting is
held.

May 18. Rail connection to Chicago is
achieved.

July 16. The Milwaukee Light Guard, a militia company of native born citizens, is organized by Rufus King.

July 21. The _Allegheny_, the first screw steamer built in Milwaukee, is launched.

September 10. The Milwaukee Police Department, eleven patrolmen paid thirty dollars each month, is created.

Fall. Christopher Bach organizes the symphony orchestra he will conduct for the next fifty years.

October 4. William Beck, a former New York City policeman, becomes police chief. He will serve for fourteen of the next seventeen years and begin a tradition of politics-free police work.

October 24. Gustaff Pfiel attempts to cremate his wife's body, but a mob prevents him from perpetrating "the horror."

November 26. The Wisconsin street lighthouse is sold as a new one at North Point goes into operation.

December 23. The Milwaukee House Hotel, built by Juneau and Martin, burns down.

1856   January 16. The Milwaukee Board of Trade is organized.

March. Mayor Cross is reelected. Two annexations (March 18, October 11) add three square miles to Milwaukee in 1856.

July 19. The _Dean Richmond_ leaves Milwaukee with the first direct shipment of wheat from any Great Lakes port to Europe. In another business note, Joseph Schlitz takes over operation of the August Krug Brewery.

August. John Plankinton and James Layton open the first Milwaukee cattle market, an aid to their packing company.

October 5. Two Jewish congregations merge to form B'ne Jeshurun, Milwaukee's greatest synagogue.

October. A dance academy is opened by Professor L. W. Vizay.

November 14. Solomon Juneau dies in Theresa, Wisconsin, and his body is returned to Milwaukee for reburial on November 28.

1857   January-February. Fanny Kemble gives a series of dramatic readings from Shakespeare.

March. Mayor Cross is reelected. Increasing tax rates and the enormous city debt foster the Albany Hall Movement to obtain charter revision and oust the aldermanic "tax eaters."

March 31. A ninth ward is created.

April 15. The Milwaukee and Mississippi Railroad reaches the Mississippi at Prairie du Chien, but the road is in deep financial trouble.

Summer. L. J. Higby opens Milwaukee's first grain elevator (50,000 bushel capacity).

July 27. A new city hall is dedicated in the Cross Block, but it is soon disclosed that Mayor Cross has increased rent charges sevenfold.

July 29. The Milwaukee Y.M.C.A. is organized with 116 charter members.

August. Newhall House, the "show hotel" of the Northwest, is opened.

The Panic of 1857 severely affects the iron industry and the many competing railroads; it also destroys Milwaukee's credit.

November 17. As city bonds fall to half value, reform groups gather in Albany Hall to unite on a political ticket that will grant tax relief.

December. The four year "straight cut" project is completed. Lake traffic now has easy access to the inner harbor and the Milwaukee River, but the cost to the city has been almost half a million dollars.

1858   January 12. An investigatory report of the

Cross Administration is issued by the Albany Hall reformers; Milwaukee owes a debt of $2,500,000 on an assessed valuation of barely $6,000,000.

January. The first public high school opens, and a second follows in September.

March 27. The legislature approves a revision of the charter which creates a bi-cameral (aldermen and councilors) city government, limits city taxing power to $175,000 yearly, and somewhat strengthens the mayor's office.

April 6. William Prentiss is elected mayor as Albany Hall sweeps the elections. Only eight members of the old council win reelection as Milwaukee reforms its government.

May 13. A Wisconsin senate investigation describes how Byron Kilbourn manipulated funds and bribed officials to build his railroads. The depression and these revelations shatter Kilbourn's career.

May 28. The Milwaukee Bar Association is approved by the legislature -- it first meets on October 23.

May 31. The lake/river thaw covers Milwaukee's docks and causes severe flooding in the city.

August 2. Delegates to a charter convention are elected in Milwaukee.

August 17. Milwaukee celebrates completion of the Atlantic cable.

August 22. Rail connection to LaCrosse is completed.

October 21. The Milwaukee Chamber of Commerce is organized and immediately wins approval for a new system of inspecting, weighing and grading of grain exports.

November 3. The Third Ward is completely flooded by the Milwaukee River.

November 22. The Chamber of Commerce officially opens.

December. Milwaukee's rail subsidies peak at $1,614,000; all but $200,000 will ultimately be repaid, but prospects in this depression year are bleak, and many city property owners fail to pay their taxes.

1859   January 1. A federal customs house opens.

January 7. A board of supervisors of the poor is appointed.

January 18. Milwaukee Scotsmen organize the St. Andrew's (benevolent) Society.

February 1. The work of the charter convention is rejected, 1,093-392, because it appears to repudiate all city debts.

March 8. The Northwestern Mutual Life Insurance Co. relocates itself in Milwaukee.

March 17. The Unitarian Society opens the Church of the Redeemer.

March 18. Milwaukee's first municipal court is created.

April. The Sisters of Charity open St. Mary's Hospital.

Herman L. Page is elected mayor -- the Albany Hall reform movement lasted only one year.

May 1. The council approves the conversion of the Old Market House into a city hall.

May. Rufus King becomes Milwaukee's first superintendent of schools.

May 30. The first street car line is authorized.

June 21. Young's Block again burns to the ground.

July 13. A mass meeting calls for the end of free running animals in Milwaukee streets.

July. The Irish City Guard is ordered to disband and reorganizes as the Union (Barry) Guards.

September 30. Abraham Lincoln speaks on

farm problems at the Wisconsin State Fair
held in Milwaukee.

November. The Philharmonic Society is organized to compete with Balatka's Music So-
city, but it lasts only five months.

1860   January. The two high schools are closed,
and are replaced with Normal classes.

February. Justice Erastus Foote of the Municipal Court is declared to hold office il-
legally. His replacement, James Mallory,
will dispense rapid justice for the next
twenty-nine years.

April 1. William Lynde, a former Democratic
congressman, is elected mayor but the Republican party elects the treasurer, its
first city official.

April 5. Rufus King organizes Milwaukee's
first baseball team, the "Cream City Club,"
whose successor will join the National League
in 1878.

May 30. The River and Lake Shore Railway
line begins horsecar operation.

July. The Milwaukee Brewing Association is
established; the city has over 200 saloons.

September 8. The Lady Elgin transports hundreds of Milwaukeeans to Chicago on an outing
to raise funds for the Union Guards. On its
return trip, it is rammed by a lumber schooner
and 300-400 lives are lost.

October. Hans Balatka of the Music Society
becomes director of the Chicago Philharmonic
Orchestra.

November. Abraham Lincoln carries Wisconsin,
but loses Milwaukee by 901 votes.

December 30. All city hall records are destroyed in a warehouse fire.

Milwaukee's population reaches 45,246, but
it has fallen far behind Chicago. Its ethnic
composition is illustrated by its total of
four English and four German newspapers.

1861   January 18. The Milwaukee and Mississippi
             Railroad is sold and reorganized.

             March 2. Seven years after fugitive slave
             Glover was freed and after interminable
             court cases, Sherman Booth receives a presi-
             dential pardon.

             March 5. John Nazio, a hardware dealer, es-
             tablishes the Milwaukee Merchants Associa-
             tion.

             March 19. Milwaukee is bankrupt with a debt
             of $2,800,000. The Wisconsin legislature
             approves the Readjustment Act which provides
             for long-term debt funding and creates a
             three member public debt commission (named in
             April) to manage the city debt. Ten years
             of gradual economic recovery follow the crea-
             tion of the commission.

             April 3. In a show of Union loyalty, both
             parties nominate James S. Brown as mayor.

             April 23. The Milwaukee Light Guard is part
             of the first Wisconsin Regiment to train at
             Camp Scott outside the city. Milwaukee ul-
             timately supplies four generals, twenty-one
             colonels and 5,000 soldiers to the Union
             war effort. Over 1,000 Milwaukee men will
             be killed or wounded.

             May. The Edward P. Allis Co. is created, the
             start of a machinery empire.

             June 24. Milwaukee undergoes the "Bank Riot"
             after the State and Mitchell banks refused
             to honor greenbacks from ten other banks.
             Troops are mobilized to end the disturbances,
             but both banks are wrecked.

             September 8. A mob lynches a black, Marshall
             Clark, who had been involved in the murder
             of an Irishman.

             October 14. William Beck resigns as chief
             of police.

             November 6. Milwaukee's first steam fire
             engine, the "Solomon Juneau," goes into
             service.

             Winter. In an effort to meet draft quotas,

a bounty payment system for volunteers is instituted by the wards of the city.

1862   March 1. Albany Hall is destroyed by fire.

April. Regular Democrat Horace Chase is elected mayor.

July 11. Clinton Walworth is appointed the first police justice.

July. A chamber of commerce drive nets $12,000 to raise a Milwaukee regiment.

July 31. Kneelands Grove is the site of a war rally by 30,000 Wisconsinites.

September. Milwaukee suffers an Indian scare, and hundreds of farmers take shelter in the city after reports of the New Ulm (Minnesota) massacre.

October 6. The Twenty-sixth Wisconsin Regiment, two-thirds composed of Milwaukee Germans, leaves for the war.

November 19. The draft law goes into operation without any demonstrations. Lincoln issues a call for five additional Wisconsin regiments.

December. Milwaukee passes Chicago and ranks as the largest primary wheat market in the world. Port traffic soars from 25,844 tons during 1862 to 140,771 tons in 1863.

1863   January 1. Camp Reno, on the northeast side of Milwaukee, burns down and three soldiers die.

February 3. The new chamber of commerce offices are dedicated.

April. Edward O'Neill of County Kilkenny is elected mayor without opposition. He reappoints William Beck as police chief.

May 5. Alexander Mitchell organizes the Milwaukee and St. Paul Railroad to handle the wheat trade. By 1869, this road controls all through routes in Wisconsin from the Lake to the Mississippi.

John Plankinton dissolves his partnership with Layton and takes Philip Armour into his packing company.

August 3. Milwaukee Hospital, founded by Dr. W. Passavent, opens.

The first Polish Catholic church in Milwaukee, St. Stanislaus, is organized.

November. The second wartime draft goes into operation.

1864   January. Arthur MacArthur is promoted to major for bravery at the Battle of Missionary Ridge; his conduct is rewarded with the Congressional Medal of Honor.

March. The Milwaukee Soldier's Home opens.

April 5. Abner Kirby, an eccentric hotel-keeper, is elected mayor, and in his inaugural speech denounces Lincoln.

Marquette College obtains a charter, but instruction does not begin until 1881.

September 19. The third wartime draft begins, and the city meets its quota by January, 1865.

November. George McClellan wins two-thirds of Milwaukee's presidential vote, but Lincoln carries Wisconsin.

The business event of the year passed almost unnoticed; Philip Best accepted his son-in-law, Captain Frederick Pabst, as a partner in his brewing firm.

1865   January 1. A letter carrier system is inaugurated.

January 4. A 13.7 acre park honors the memory of Solomon Juneau.

January 31. The Music Hall, constructed by the Music Society at a cost of $65,000, is dedicated. It becomes the Academy of Music in 1869.

March 2. The State Bank of Wisconsin becomes the Milwaukee National Bank.

April. John Talmadge, an Independent Democrat, is elected mayor. The welcome he ac-
cords returning soldiers wins universal
plaudits.

April 24. A house numbering system goes into effect.

May. Frederick Pomeroy is named Superintendent of schools.

May 29. A twenty-five year franchise to the
Milwaukee City Railway Co. goes into effect.

June. Sherburn Merrill becomes general manager of the Milwaukee and St. Paul and
slowly increases Milwaukee's rail trade.

June 28. The Soldiers Home Fair raises over
$100,000 by featuring attractions such as
"Old Abe," the eagle mascot of the 8th
Wisconsin. Congress is impressed and later
authorizes one of four national veterans
homes in Milwaukee.

December. Statistics show that Milwaukee
exported over 60,000,000 bushels of wheat
and 13,000,000 barrels of flour during the
war. The city ranks as the largest grain
port and the greatest flour milling center
in the West. Its population grew twenty-
three per cent during the war years.

1866   March. The case of Gillespie v. Palmer af-
firms the right of blacks to vote in Milwaukee and some twenty-five to thirty do so at
the next election.

April 4. The Rock River Dam breaks. No
lives are lost but flood damage is extensive,
and the Humbolt Street bridge is destroyed.

April. Talmadge is reelected mayor as a
Republican supporter of congressional recon-
struction. Congress approves $48,283 for
harbor improvements.

April 12. Milwaukee's first house of correc-
tion opens.

June 30. A public meeting is held to plan
for an immigrant reception center.

The Milwaukee and St. Paul Railroad opens
Union Depot.

September 10. Tamarack Street is renamed
State Street.

September 20. George Walker dies, the only
one of the three major city pioneers to die
in Milwaukee.

Fall 1866-1867. The bluff at Wisconsin
Street, original site of the Milwaukee lighthouse is torn down and the earth used as
landfill for the expanding city.

November. An orphans shelter, The Home of
the Friendless, opens.

1867   March 7. Newell Daniels organizes city
            shoemakers into the Knights of St. Crispin.

            April. Edward O'Neill is again elected mayor.

            April 11. The state legislature approves a
            five-man Milwaukee Board of Health. James
            Johnson is appointed chairman, and he orders
            slaughterhouse regulation.

            May 1. The Northwest Branch of the National
            Soldier's Home opens in Milwaukee.

            May-October. A charter convention meets, but
            almost all of their recommendations will be
            defeated in 1868.

            November. Carl Schurz visits Milwaukee and
            discovers an "extra-ordinary amount of build-
            ing and of a very high order of beauty."

1868   January. Milwaukee's first permanent high
            school opens in the Seventh Ward.

            April. Edward O'Neill overwhelmingly defeats
            Republican John Plankinton and retains the
            mayoralty. Plankinton is somewhat soothed
            when his new hotel opens.

            April 8. The town of Bay View is established.

            June 23. The patent for America's first type-
            writer is issued to C. C. Scholes, Carlos
            Glidden and Samuel Soule, who constructed the
            machine during 1867. Today the Museum

of Natural and Human History in Milwaukee
contains the world's finest display of these
instruments. Scholes, the prime inventor,
ultimately sells his interests to Remington
and Sons (1873).

September-November. An epidemic of over 500
reported cases of smallpox forces the closing
of all schools.

October 21. The Stadt Theater, a German
playhouse, opens. Recognizing the ethnic
nature of Milwaukee, the school board approves German language study as part of the
curriculum. By 1870, forty-six per cent of
all Milwaukee students will formally study
the language.

1869   February. A box fire alarm system goes into
operation.

February 24-25. A woman's suffrage convention
is held in Old City Hall.

April. O'Neill is reelected mayor without
opposition. The voters approve creation of
a board of public works (named by the mayor
with council approval) to improve public
buildings, sewers, bridges, docks, etc. Milwaukee's most pressing need is a sewer system, for the city literally stinks. Landfill operations to convert Menomonee River
swampland into solid ground begin.

July 5. The Milwaukee Old Settler's Club is
organized.

September 30. Temple Emanu-El, Milwaukee's
first Reform Jewish Congregation, is formed
when dissidents withdraw from B'ne Jeshurun.

October 8. A trades union group, the Labor
Reform Assembly, is organized.

November 1. The cornerstone of All Saints
Cathedral (Episcopal) is set in place.

November 5. The Gaiety Theater burns to the
ground.

December. The value of Milwaukee manufacturing is $18,798,122. Dominant in the growing
iron and machinery field is the E. P. Allis

Co. and the three-man board of public works
awards Allis a contract for iron sewer pipe,
despite the fact that the company possesses
no pipe-producing machinery. This over-
sight is quickly remedied.

WISCONSIN METROPOLIS
1870-1909

1870   Milwaukee has a population of 71,440 people
in thirteen square miles. Germans compose a
third of the total, but for the first time
a majority of the population is American born
(fifty-three per cent).

April. Joseph Phillips becomes Milwaukee's
mayor, the fifteenth Democrat among the first
sixteen mayors. His narrow margin of victory
presages the next forty years of city politics during which the two major parties will
divide twenty-two elections.

April 11. Main Street is renamed Broadway.

Summer. Alexander Mitchell, president of two
railroads and the city's richest resident
(about twenty million dollars) builds a mansion.

November 1. Increase Lapham's lifetime project becomes reality as the U. S. Signal Service begins to operate; today it is the U. S.
Weather Bureau.

November 11. Best & Co. (Pabst) purchases
Melms Brewery.

December. Milwaukee wheat exports reach
16,127,838 bushels and 1,225,941 barrels of
flour. William J. Langson has inaugurated
"The Pit" to handle wheat dealings.

1871   March 24. The Wisconsin legislature gives
Milwaukee authority to construct a water
works designed by Chicago engineer, E. S.
Chesborough. The city issues $1,600,000 in
seven per cent bonds to build the project.

April. Milwaukee elects Harrison Ludington
mayor on the People's Ticket (Republican).
His inaugural address calls for fewer taxes
and more manufacturing.

May 27-29. "Germantown" celebrates Prussia's victory in her war against France.

Summer-Fall. A severe smallpox epidemic causes almost 300 deaths.

August 17. Jacob and Herman Nunnemacher open their Grand Opera House, a "perfect theater," with a performance of <u>Martha</u>.

September 7. Construction begins on a new court house upon the site of Juneau's original gift to the city.

December. Milwaukee is the largest tanning center in the world and the fourth largest meat packer in America; beer exports soar to 142,000 barrels. In 1872, when fifty per cent of all beer is exported, much of it goes south to Chicago where the breweries were destroyed in the great fire.

1872   March 31. A tenth ward is added to Milwaukee; three others are created by 1874.

April. Democrat David Hooker is elected mayor when Ludington chooses not to run for reelection.

Henry C. Payne organizes the Young Men's Republican Club.

July 4. A freak snowstorm strikes Milwaukee.

Summer-Fall. Smallpox kills 217 residents of the city.

August 25. The Blatz Brewery burns down.

August 30. In an effort to service the many Jewish immigrants from the Chicago fire, Congregation Emanu-El opens a new Synagogue.

September 19. Congregation B'ne Jeshurun opens a new synagogue.

1873   January 22. A municipal courthouse of red sandstone, designed by Leonard Schmidtner, opens.

April. Levi Kellogg, a member of the common council, is elected mayor by 217 votes. However, he is declared ineligible by virtue

of his position in the council and in a special election he loses to Ludington.

July 17. The Episcopal Cathedral of All
Saints is consecrated.

Summer-Fall. Only 114 smallpox deaths are
reported, the best record in three years.

A kindergarten opens in the German Academy.
Another weekly German language newspaper,
Germania, begins to publish.

September. The Panic of 1873 strikes Milwaukee. Although not a single bank fails,
the depression seriously injures the labor
movement in the city.

October 24. The first water works plant is
completed.

1874   February. Alexander Mitchell's Milwaukee and
St. Paul Railroad becomes the Chicago, Milwaukee and St. Paul, the famous "Milwaukee
Road." It soon revolutionizes Wisconsin's
dairy industry by introducing refrigerated
cars.

March. A paid fire department is authorized.

April. Harrison Ludington defeats Edward
O'Neill and remains mayor. A revised charter
goes into operation; it creates a unicameral
council, thirty-nine aldermen serving three-
year staggered terms. The treasurer, comptroller and city attorney posts remain elective, as does the school board. The mayor's
office remains weak, having little authority
over city services and dispensing only meager patronage.

May. James MacAlister becomes superintendent
of schools. He immediately creates a teachers
library and reforms the schools so thoroughly
that Milwaukee wins national honors at the
Philadelphia Exposition (1876).

June 1. The West Side Street Railway is incorporated and begins to run horsecars on
June 11.

The Krug Brewery becomes the Joseph Schlitz
Brewing Company.

August 7. The Robert Burns Club is formed.

September 14. The North Point pumping station delivers its first water from Lake Michigan to Milwaukee homes.

December. The ten railroads that serve Milwaukee carried 32,500,000 bushels of grain to the city during the year.

1875   February 12. Milwaukee is made an archbishopric of the Catholic Church.

April. Ludington is again elected Mayor.

May 2. The temperature falls to 25 degrees below zero.

May 9. Joseph Schlitz dies in the sinking of an ocean liner off Ireland. His name will be immortalized by his successors, the Uihlein Brothers, who produce the "Beer that made Milwaukee Famous." In 1875, however, it is Valentine Blatz who produces the first bottled beer and he wins the Philadelphia Exposition prize in 1876.

July 1. Milwaukee's waterworks are turned over to the Board of Public Works for municipal operation.

September. The Milwaukee Musical School and Society is established.

September 14. Increase Lapham, Milwaukee's greatest scholar and "Father of the U. S. Weather Bureau," dies.

December 27. Henry Benjamin becomes acting mayor when Ludington resigns to become governor of Wisconsin.

1876   Ammi R. Butler, allied with Milwaukee's Democratic boss John Hinsey, is elected Milwaukee's first two-year mayor.

May. The Socialist begins to publish.

July. The "Whiskey Ring" cases are finally concluded; Jacob Nunnemacher is the most prominent Milwaukee man convicted. He is fined $10,000 and serves two months in jail before President Ulysses S. Grant pardons him.

October 13. Rufus King, editor, educator
and civic leader, dies.

December 18. Spring Street is renamed Grand
Avenue.

December 22. The permanent structure of the
Y.M.C.A. is created as several city groups
are reorganized.

1877   April. The Milwaukee Workingman's Party e-
lects two aldermen, two supervisors and two
constables while polling 1500 votes.

May 5. The Life Saving Station opens.

The firm of Wolf and Davidson opens the
port's first fully equipped dry dock.

The first telephone switchboard opens with
fifteen subscribers.

October 15. Milwaukee City Hospital opens.

November 20. The Arion Musical Chorus is organized.

1878   February 7. The Milwaukee Public Library is
authorized by act of the legislature. In
March, the Young Men's Association donates
its 10,000 volumes and lays the foundation
of the city's library system.

March. George Peck's *Sun* first appears in
Milwaukee.

March 21. Joseph Clauder establishes a symphony orchestra.

April. John Black is elected mayor by a margin of 300 votes with the help of "property-
less bummers." Council leader Thomas Brown
leads opposition to the mayor. The first
Polish officeholder, August Ridzinski, is
elected supervisor in the Twelfth Ward.

July 8. The Public Library opens.

September. The Sisters of the Poor open the
Milwaukee Home for the Aged.

As the city expands its services, arc lights
are installed on Milwaukee streets, contracts

for private garbage collections are let, and
a separate department of health is authorized.

1879   May 10. The Milwaukee Telephone Exchange,
designed by Professor C. H. Haskins, opens.

July. The Schlitz Company buys Quentin Park,
and shortly reopens it complete with a theater, zoo, and fountains. As Schlitz Park,
it accomodates up to 20,000 patrons and becomes a center of Gemutlichkeit.

November 9. The Sentinel begins to publish
a Sunday edition.

December. Milwaukee manufactures reach a
value of $43,973,812.

1880   March 21. Franz Huebschmann, a leader of
the Milwaukee German community for forty
years, dies.

April 5. Professor C. H. Haskins illuminates
Milwaukee streets with an electric light
system.

April. Republican Thomas Brown becomes the
first native Milwaukeean elected mayor.

May 8. The German Association is founded to
aid new immigrants.

June 8. The National Encampment of the Grand
Army of the Republic convenes in Milwaukee;
140,000 veterans are addressed by former
President Ulysses S. Grant. The meeting en-
hances Milwaukee's reputation and provides
enormous stimulus to city industry and
growth.

The Milwaukee Turnverein gymnastic team, led
by George Brosius, wins the world championship in competition at Frankfurt.

September. Another innovation by School Superintendent MacAlister, evening schools for
adults, goes into operation.

December. Milwaukee's population is 115,587.
The city's largest industry is not brewing
but meat packing.

1881   March 19. The winter of 1880-81 is the
                snowiest in Milwaukee's history as over ele-
                ven feet fall. At no time in February and
                March were all railroad lines operating, and
                today all street travel was suspended.

                April 21. A spring flood carries off the
                Milwaukee Dam and causes extensive flooding.
                Congress approves a breakwater across Milwau-
                kee Bay to create a harbor of refuge, although
                the work is not completed until 1909.

                September 5. Marquette College opens with
                five professors and thirty-five students.
                Its first class of five will not graduate un-
                til June 1887. Concordia College (Lutheran)
                also holds its first classes this year.

                September 6. The Milwaukee Exposition Hall
                opens; it holds annual industrial displays
                for the next twenty-one years.

                September 7. Archbishop Henni, "Patriarch of
                the Northwest," dies and is succeeded by
                Michael Heiss.

                November 15. The Lief Ericson Memorial, do-
                nated by Mrs. J. Gilbert, is dedicated.

1882   January 1. The Associated Charities of Mil-
                waukee is organized.

                March. The first public kindergarten class
                is held.

                April. John M. Stowell is elected mayor.
                Elected with the support of labor, Stowell
                loses their support when he tried to close
                all saloons, dance and concert halls at mid-
                night.

                April 13. The Wisconsin legislature allows
                Milwaukee to accept the collections of the
                Natural History Society and use them to found
                a public museum.

                June 1. The Jewish community petitions city
                aid for an unexpected influx of immigrating
                Russian Jews.

                June 29, Stowell announces that 350 Russian
                Jews are expected to arrive. Only 218 actu-
                ally land at Milwaukee, but an additional 400

arrive in the next four months.

December 11. Lucius Nieman becomes editor
of the Daily Journal.

1883   January 10. At least eighty persons die as
the Newhall Hotel, victim of thirty fires
in eight years, burns down; arson is the
suspected cause. The city mandates fire escapes on all new buildings.

February 20. The trustees for the Public Museum organize and name Charles Doerflinger
curator.

George Peck publishes Peck's Bad Boy and His
Pa, an effort once serialized in Peck's Sun.

1884   April. Berlin-born Emil Walber is elected
mayor for the first of two terms. He will
succeed in putting police and firemen under
a non-political commission.

May 24. The Public Museum opens.

Summer. The first Milwaukee Blue Book of
800 society leaders is published. The un-
doubted social leader of Milwaukee, Mrs.
Martha Mitchell, sponsors the "Kermess"
Festival of All Nations.

Plankinton and Armour is reorganized and
takes into partnership Patrick Cudahy.

1885   April 11. The Board of Fire and Police Commissioners, today the oldest civil service
agency in Wisconsin, is created.

May 11. The Daily Journal becomes the Milwaukee Journal, and, led by Nieman, it soon
will be the largest paper in Wisconsin.

Summer. Paul Zabel conducts twelve concerts
of operatic performances in Schlitz Park.

Artists at the American Panorama Co. begin
creation of massive Cyclorama paintings, including the famous "Battle of Atlanta."

September. A state Normal school is established in Milwaukee; it is the forerunner of
Wisconsin's State Teachers College.

September 28. Division Street is renamed
Juneau Avenue.

November 7. A monument to George Washington,
donated by Elizabeth Plankinton, is dedicated.

November 15. The Milwaukee Press Club is
organized.

1886

Spring. Forty strikes paralyze the city as
workers demand ten hour wages for eight hours
of work. Twelve thousand strikers are out
by May 1.

April. Walber is reelected despit frauds
"systematically planned and deliberately carried out." His Inaugural asks construction
of a new city hall and calls for public
baths and a city park system.

May 3. One thousand railway strikers raid
the West Milwaukee shops of the Milwaukee
Road and induce 1,400 workers to walk off
their jobs.

May 4. Violence erupts at the Rolling Mills
ironworks in Bay View. Five strikers die
and four others are seriously wounded when
the state militia fires into a crowd.

May 13. Governor Jeremiah Rusk orders the
militia withdrawn from Milwaukee.

May 23. Archbishop Heiss presides over the
First Provincial Council of Milwaukee, held
in St. John's Cathedral.

August 31. Milwaukee experiences a minor
earthquake.

November. Organized labor sweeps the Milwaukee County elections and elects a labor candidate to Congress. It is claimed that Milwaukee has fifty Knights of Labor Lodges with
16,000 members.

1887

March 8. The Village of Bay View (pop. 4,017)
is incorporated into Milwaukee.

April. Charter revision limits aldermanic
representation to two per ward, and reduces
terms to two years.

April 19. Alexander Mitchell, banker and railroad mogol, dies.

July. The Juneau Monument, donated by Charles Bradley, is dedicated.

September. The Gimbel Brothers Department Store opens.

1888   March. The Milwaukee labor movement is divided as Paul Grottkau organizes the Socialist Labor Party to compete with the Union Labor Party.

April. The Citizens Ticket of Republicans and Democrats elects Thomas Brown mayor over Union Labor candidate Herman Kroeger.

April 5. The Layton Art Gallery opens.

April 6. The Milwaukee Art Society is organized.

April 25. The Association for the Advancement of Milwaukee is incorporated -- and succeeds in obtaining for the city the National G.A.R. Encampment of 1888.

September 3. The Swift Brothers incorporate a dressed meat concern.

September. A flushing tunnel to the Milwaukee River is completed at a cost of $240,744. It utilizes lake water to speed the river current and thus more quickly expel the sewerage that gives the city a distinctive aroma.

October 26. Former police boss of the Milwaukee Road, John T. Janssen, becomes police commissioner, a post he holds for the next thirty-three years.

1889   March. A mob attacks Chinese workers.

March 18. The Phillip Best Company changes its name to the Pabst Brewery Co. Under the leadership of Captain Fred Pabst it becomes America's largest brewer. This summer, the company opens a resort park at Whitefish Bay, where patrons learn "He drinks Best who drinks Pabst."

April 1. Edward Allis, entrepreneur and

builder of the Corliss Engine, dies.

June 16. The board of park commissioners
first meets. Within a year they purchase
five park sites.

Auguts 26. The Twenty-third National Encampment of the Grand Army of the Republic convenes in Milwaukee.

August 29. The Bijou Opera House opens.

September. The fireboat _Cataract_ is purchased by the fire department.

October. A black wins a judgment against the
Bijou when it refuses him a seat. There are
only 494 blacks in the city.

December. Sixteen years of public works have
given the city 220 miles of improved streets
and at least forty bridges. The value of
manufactures reaches $97,503,951.

1890   The U. S. Census labels Milwaukee (pop.
204,468) the "most foreign" city in the
United States; the city is also fifty-two
per cent Catholic.

February 14. The first public bath in Milwaukee is opened.

April 1. George Peck, Democrat and creator
of "Hennery the Bad Boy," is elected mayor.
His platform condemns the Bennett Law manda-
ting that English be taught in all Wisconsin
schools.

April 3. Milwaukee's first electric trolley
begins to operate.

April 18. Republican Governor William Hoard
signs the Bennett Law, and almost all Wisconsin Germans vote Democratic in November.

July 26. Peck institutes open air concerts
in Juneau Park.

September 17. The Pabst Theater celebrates
its Grand Opening with a performance of
Egmont.

October 6. Twelve thousand Germans march in

the greatest German Day celebration ever
held.

November 17. George Peck, elected governor
on the strength of German votes, resigns
his mayoral office and is replaced by Peter
J. Somers.

December 22. The Milwaukee Street Railway
Co. is formed by Henry Villard.

December. Milwaukee's export of beer reaches
1,800,000 barrels, 700,000 of which are produced by the Pabst Co.

1891   March 4. Pabst opens a beer pipe line from
its cellars to its bottling operations, a
project that needed specific congressional
authorization.

April 30. Milwaukee annexes four square
miles to the city.

June 30. Catholic Archbishop Frederic Xavier
Katzner is installed.

November 10. Electric heaters warm the trol-
leys of the Milwaukee Street Railway.

1892   Winter-Spring. A diphtheria epidemic takes
400 lives.

March 1. A wreck in the railroad yards kills
seven people.

A park board is established to oversee not
only the park system but also future city
planning.

March. Sarah Bernhardt is poorly reviewed
in a city that still prefers German theater.

April. Peter Somers is elected mayor in his
own right after defeating an attempted im-
pachment.

Summer. Telephone ties to New York are established.

September. The Y.W.C.A. is organized.

October. A vast fire sweeps the largely
Irish third ward. Over $5,000,000 of property

across twenty-six acres is destroyed and
some 2,000 people are made homeless.

December. School teacher Victor Berger resigns his post and founds the Wisconsin Vor-
warts to preach Socialism.

Milwaukee ranks first in American tanning,
mills over 2,117,000 barrels of flour, and
exports over a million barrels of beer
through the Pabst Co. alone.

1893   March. John L. Mitchell takes his seat in
the U. S. Senate.

April 10. Fourteen men drown in a construction crib as the North Point water intake is
built.

May. The Wisconsin College of Physicians
and Surgeons is incorporated. Its first
classes are held in October.

June. Mayor Somers wins a special election
for the House of Representatives, where he
replaces John Mitchell. Republican merchant John Koch becomes mayor.

June-July. The Panic of 1893 forces five
Milwaukee banks to close -- three never re-
open.

August 22. Unemployed workers demonstrate
for jobs, but few injuries are reported.

October. Milwaukee Medical College is incorporated.

November. Pabst Beer is awarded the World
Columbian Exposition Prize at Chicago.

Milwaukeean Charles K. Harris publishes "After the Ball." Among his other song hits
will be "Heaven will Protect the Working
Girl" and "Hello Central, Give me Heaven."

1894   January. Henry C. Payne merges all Milwaukee trolley lines into a transit monopoly.

February 24. The cornerstone of a new city
hall (designed by Henry Koch) is set in
place.

April. Mayor Koch is reelected.

The Stadt Theater begins to alternate English
and German plays.

April 6. The Milwaukee Baptist Church Union
is formed.

April 9. Nine firemen die in a balze at the
Davidson Theater.

Fall-Winter. Smallpox kills 244 persons.
The epidemic continues into 1895 when over
1000 cases are reported with 268 deaths.

1895   February 22. Milwaukee's ladies clubs utilize
the _Journal's_ plant and print a charity edition on silk stock paper.

April. The Wisconsin legislature approves a
non-partisan civil service system for Milwaukee. Chairman Joseph Stark organizes the
commission on June 20.

June 27. Milwaukee College merges with
Downer College. Miss Ellen C. Sabin will
serve as president of the new institution
until 1921.

September 25. The North Point intake, 3,146
feet of tube into Lake Michigan, is completed
after twenty lives have been lost in its construction.

November 8. A new Pabst Theater, designed by
Otto Straach without interior columns or sup-
ports, opens to house Milwaukee's German
Theater.

November 18. The Polish Association of A-
merica is organized in Milwaukee. The city
also receives this year its first appreciable
number of Sicilian immigrants.

December 10. The Parkman Club for historical
investigation is founded.

December 23. Inauguration ceremonies are
held to open the new city hall; its 393-
foot bell tower dominates the city skyline.

1896   January 29. The Milwaukee Electric Railway
and Light Co., a monopoly led by William C.

Nelson (N.Y.C.) and Henry Payne, is organized.

March. Milwaukee organizes its nineteenth, twentieth, and twenty-first wards.

April. William Rauschenberger, a Prussian-born cordage manufacturer, is elected mayor on the Republican ticket.

April 10. Mrs. Emil Schandein presents Carl Von Marr's painting Flagellants to the city of Milwaukee.

May 3-June. The Amalgamated Street Railways Employees Union goes out on strike demanding union recognition and a penny raise to twenty cents an hour. Chief Janssen allows his policemen to act as switchtenders and to use their guns to protect streetcars. With his help Payne breaks the strike and then refuses to rehire the strikers.

The city decides to repave all its streets with granite, brick or asphalt, a project that causes much graft for the next decade.

1897   A year of business prosperity. A car ferry to Ludington, Michigan, is begun by the Chesapeake and Ohio Railroad. Julian Simon opens the Boston Store for discriminating shoppers, and a citizens business league is organized to preach the advantages of Milwaukee and to obatin conventions. Over 900 conventions meet in Milwaukee in the next decade, their participants drawn not only for business but also for the carnal pleasures of River Street. The only jarring note, of minor importance to businessmen, was the organization of Branch #1 of the Social Democratic Party of America in Milwaukee's Ethical Hall (July 9, 1897).

1898   January. Pabst "Blue Ribbon" beer is first marketed.

March 17. The outgoing city council approves construction of a muncipally owned garbage treatment plant.

April 5. David "All the time Rosy" Rose is elected mayor, defeating both a Socialist and a Republican he labeled "servant" to the

"streetcar monopoly." Once elected, Rose
makes common cause with aldermen in support
of franchise privileges, and against civil
service regulations

An interurban transit line goes into operation
between Milwaukee and its suburbs. The Edward
Allis Co., forseeing the suburban future, purchases land to build a company town which today, as West Allis, is Wisconsin's fourth
largest city.

June 12. Milwaukeeans found the Wisconsin
Archeological Society.

June 28. The Soldier's Monument, paid for
by popular subscription, is dedicated.

August 30. The first outdoor concerts in
Washington Park are held.

1899   January 23. The Museum and Library Building
on Grand Avenue is completed after five years
of work and $630,000 in costs.

April 22. The new federal post office opens.

May 18. George Odenbrett operates the first
automobile seen in Milwaukee.

December. Milwaukee ends the century as a
great city. Its population has soared forty
per cent since 1890 and the value of its
manufactures has reached $123,786,449.

1900   January 2. Despite public outcry, Mayor Rose
and twenty-five of forty-two aldermen approve
a thirty-four year city franchise for the
Milwaukee Electric Railway and Light Co.;
Rose signs the bill ignoring both a court
injunction and its increased fare provisions.

January 29. The American Baseball League is
founded and Milwaukee's "Cream City Club,"
led by Connie Mack, finishes second. The
team falls to last place in 1901 and is
dropped from the league.

April. Rose, supported by utility and liquor
interests, and utilizing his patronage machine, narrowly wins election over Republican
Henry Baumgaertner. The voters approve a
municipally owned electric light plant. In

his inaugural speech, Rose recommends a vast
harbor improvement plan.

December. Milwaukee's population has quad-
rupled in thirty years to 285,315. The city
remains seventy-two per cent of Germanic origin, but most Germans are now native born.
The Black population is only 862, .3 per
cent of the total.

1901   February 18. Charles Pfister purchases the
            Sentinel.

            March 11. The Allis-Chalmers Co. is formed
            when four companies, all producers of heavy
            equipment, merge. Some 5,000 workers are
            employed at their five plants, and the new
            corporation begins to construct a scientifi-
            cally designed manufacturing plant in West
            Allis.

            A juvenile court is established for Milwaukee.

1902   January. Henry Payne becomes postmaster
            general of the United States.

            David Adler organizes the Federated Jewish
            Charities.

            March 18. Horatio Wells, one of Milwaukee's
            pioneers and its second mayor, dies.

            April. Milwaukee becomes a charter member
            of the American Association Baseball League,
            but its Brewers win only eight pennants be-
            fore the league is abolished in 1963.

            "All the time Rosy" Rose is reelected mayor
            despite his opposition to any restrictions
            on utility power or River Street vice. How-
            ever, his Socialist opponent receives 8,400
            votes.

            December. Schlitz surpasses Pabst to become
            Milwaukee's (and America's) largest brewer.

1903   April. A municipally-owned garbage incinera-
            tor, five years under construction, goes into
            operation.

            September. The Milwaukee School of Engineer-
            ing, a private, nonprofit institution, opens.

September 28. A mass meeting demands a grand jury investigation of the Rose Adminis- tration. Ultimately, seventy-four indict- ments will be handed down and thirty-six convictions will be obtained. Mayor Rose, however, escapes untouched.

November 29. The Reverend Sebastian Messmer is named Catholic Archbishop of Milwaukee, and is installed on December 10.

1904   January 1. Colonel Frederick Pabst dies.

January. Milwaukee becomes one of the first American cities to offer a four year commer- cial high school diploma. However, only 4.2 per cent of eligible pupils attend any high school.

February. The non-partisan Voters League is organized.

April. Although thirty-three indictments have already been issued against his ap- pointees, David Rose is elected mayor for the fourth time, with 23,515 votes. His oppo- nets included Guy Goff, a La Follette Re- publican (17,598 votes), Socialist Victor Berger (15,056) and Socialist Laborite C. Witke (3,374).

The Milwaukee Council enacts a school lunch program, an anti-spitting ordinance, and one of the first laws against industrial smoke pollution.

November 7. The Milwaukee _Journal_ proves an advertising rate conspiracy case against three of its competitors and wins a judgment from the U. S. Supreme Court.

1905   January 14. The great Melba appears in Mil- waukee.

March 9. The Tenement Commission reports that the city has no identifiable tenement district, although it concedes that some city housing needs renovation.

March 22. The city cracks down on gamb- ling, and some slot machines are destroyed. Milwaukee is extraordinarily well policed, however, with only one murder and six burglaries reported during all of 1905.

June 4. The Industrial Exposition Building burns down. Fire Chief Thomas Clancy begins twenty-one years of service to Milwaukee.

June 19. A statue of Thaddeus Kosciusko, donated by the Polish community, is dedicated.

The Franklin Park Zoo opens.

1906   March. The Gargoyle Restaurant, Milwaukee's finest, opens for business.

April. Rose loses the mayoralty to twenty-nine year old "Boy Mayor" Sherburn M. Becker, while a Socialist candidate, William Arnold, receives twenty-five per cent of the vote. Becker's campaign, managed by Bill Hooker, was a wild extravaganza of parades and stunts. The showmanship continued after the election as Becker and the city attorney destroyed all standing street clocks, and the mayor drove his $3,800 Pope-Toledo roadster to visit President Roosevelt at Sagamore Hill.

July 10. The first motion picture theater opens.

Edna Ferber joins the staff of the Milwaukee Journal.

October. The council approves a Historical Museum to be constructed as part of the new Public Museum.

1907   April 1. The eleven member Metropolitan Park Commission is created due to the efforts of Alfred C. Clas; its members are appointed in July.

April. Voters approve a board of estimate and reduce the number of aldermen from forty-six to thirty-five.

May. Milwaukee Medical College is incorporated by Marquette which has been granted University status.

October 28. America's first interurban electric train leaves Milwaukee for Cedarburg, Wisconsin.

1908   April. The Majestic Theater opens, bringing burlesque to Milwaukee.

April 7. David Rose, returning from an Arizona exile, is elected mayor for the fifth time. Emil Seidel (Socialist) trails him by fewer than 3,000 votes.

June 1. The Milwaukee Municipal Reference Library is established.

June. A convention to reform the city charter meets -- and finds itself opposed by Mayor Rose.

August 12. Captain Jack Dallas makes a dirigible flight around Milwaukee and brings the city into the air age.

1909   February 13. Five firemen die as the Johns-Mansville Co. burns down.

The Wisconsin Assembly refuses to approve a "home rule" charter for Milwaukee.

June 26. John Gregory presents the Robert Burns Monument to the city. The Milwaukee Club is also founded this year.

July 4. The Milwaukee Road establishes through freight traffic to the west coast, the only railroad operating from Chicago to the Pacific on its own tracks.

Mrs. Lauren Sherry founds the Wisconsin Players, and begins the "little theater" movement in America.

July 27. Frederick Law Olmsted and John Nolan issue a planners report for a Milwaukee civic center.

The school board approves the teaching of Polish in public elementary schools.

September 21. The Milwaukee Auditorium, an 8,000 seat arena, opens on the site of the old Exhibition Hall.

December. Milwaukee reports its greatest decade of industrial growth with manufactures valued at $208,323,630. Although the city ranks as the third largest flour miller in

America, its future is better indicated by
Ole Evinrude's invention this year of an
effective outboard motor. Engines and machinery soon surpass all other Milwaukee
industries.

THE SOCIALIST ERA
1910-1939

1910   City population is reported as 373,857 people
living in twenty-three square miles. The
population of foreign born is only thirty
per cent, but fifty-three per cent of the
population is still of Germanic origin.

March 27. After fifty years of musical service to Milwaukee, Christopher Bach gives
his farewell concert.

April 5. Emil Seidel is elected the first
Socialist mayor of Milwaukee; his margin of
7,000 votes is the largest plurality in city
annals. A wood carver and former alderman,
Seidel also obtains a Social Democratic majority on the city council; his private sec-
retary is Journal reporter Carl Sandburg.
Socialist rule does not greatly change Milwaukee due to its long-term franchise agree-
ments, its debt limitations, and the opposition of legislative conservatives.

The Metropolitan Park Commission increases
its city planning operations,and Milwaukee
river beautification projects are implemented.

May 12. A new city incinerator goes into
operation. The council also orders sanitary
inspection of factories and approves the
purchase of street flushing equipment.

June 10. Chlorine is first used in the Milwaukee Water System, and the council abolishes
the public drinking cup.

Mayor Seidel's attempt to force the resigna-
tion of Police Chief Janssen ends when he is
told to "go to hell" by Janssen.

September 16. Milwaukee's first airplane
flight ends when the plane flies directly
into a grandstand, injuring eight persons.

The state supreme court voids a Socialist
plan to finance a municipally owned electric
light company.

October. The mayor creates a Bureau of Economy and Efficiency headed by University of
Wisconsin Professor John Commons. The bureau
will issue nineteen reports before the end
of 1911 and vastly aid a general reorganiza-
tion of municipal finance and administration.

November 8. Socialists gain control of the
Milwaukee County government. Victor Berger
becomes the first Socialist elected to congress.

December. Milwaukee has imported 48,000,000
bushels of grain, largely for the breweries
which produce 3,700,000 barrels in 1910.
The flour milling industry has begun to fail,
but the importation of 5,000,000 tons of
coal foreshadows the fact that by 1913 Milwaukee will rank as the greatest coal dis-
tributor on the Great Lakes.

1911   March. Mayor Seidel's Citizens Committee on
Unemployment becomes the Free Employment
Bureau. In the next three months it obtains
1,100 jobs for Milwaukee citizens.

The Socialists run an honest administration
and improve the park system. However, their
plans for municipal slaughterhouses, docks,
coal yards and ice plants all fail. A successful attack on River Street vice has the
unforseen effect of reducing tourist trade.

Summer. For the second straight year Milwaukee has many typhoid cases due to its inadequate water facilities.

October 23. The Board of Harbor Commissioners
(advisory to the mayor) is created with William Bruce as president.

December 7. Victor Berger's Social Democratic
Herald is changed to a daily, The Milwaukee
Leader -- "Unawed by influence, unbribed by
gain."

A winter street railway strike wins support
from Mayor Seidel who appoints strikers as
deputies to keep the peace.

1912   February 1. The 24th and 25th Wards of Mil-
                     waukee are created.

                     February. City Attorney Daniel Hoan brings
                     suit to force street railways to pave between
                     their tracks as a condition to keeping their
                     franchises. After Hoan wins four cases, the
                     utilities comply. Hoan also begins condemna-
                     tion proceedings against Jones Island marsh-
                     land where the administration hopes to create
                     better municipal harbor facilities.

                     April 2. Gerhard Bading is elected mayor
                     (non-partisan) with both Democratic and Re-
                     publican support. A Pole, Louis Kotecki, is
                     elected comptroller, a post he will hold un-
                     til 1933. Daniel Hoan is reelected city at-
                     torney.

                     May 6. The Wisconsin Legislature approves a
                     non-partisan election bill which removes par-
                     ty designations from the Milwaukee ballot
                     and decrees a final election between the two
                     highest vote getters.

                     Summer. In an effort to end juvenile delin-
                     quency, the Schlitz Pavilion is turned into
                     a community center, and Milwaukee establishes
                     the first Department for Directed Play in the
                     nation.

                     August 23. The Milwaukee Electric Railway
                     and Light Co. is ordered to maintain the
                     nickel fare.

                     September. Robert Cooley wins his fight for
                     vocational training and a vocational high
                     school opens under his direction.

                     September 5. Lieutenant General Arthur Mac-
                     Arthur dies while delivering a speech to a
                     G.A.R. meeting.

                     September 12. The first National Safety
                     Congress convenes in Milwaukee.

                     October 14. John Schrank attempts to assas-
                     sinate Theodore Roosevelt who proceeds to
                     deliver a fifty-page, eighty-minute speech
                     before a stunned audience.

                     November. Hoan begins legal proceedings to
                     force the Electric Company (run by John Beggs)

to pave one foot outside their tracks.

1913   January 1. Mayor Bading names the Bureau of Municipal Research to act as "the Mayor's eye" and create a more efficient government.

February 13. The Harbor Commission meets for the first time.

April 14. The Municipal Research Bureau asks the New York Municipal Bureau to report on Milwaukee's shortcomings. Among their recommendations were the end of street "bubblies" (drinking fountains), a new street sign system and a "home rule" charter.

Spring. The state mandates a sewerage commission to deal with the problem of river and lake pollution.

The city creates a nine-member non-compensated motion picture board to pass on the suitability of films for Milwaukee viewers; the board endures until 1970.

Sivyer House, oldest brick home in Milwaukee is demolished.

July. The Clauder Band begins summer concerts in the parks.

October 12. A new harbor commission is appointed by Mayor Bading.

October 26. The Goodyear Rubber Co. burns, and nine firemen die.

December. Iron and steel production ranks as Milwaukee's largest industry (46.5 million dollars), followed by leather, meat packing, and beer. Port coal traffic has trebled since 1910.

The first community Christmas tree is lit in the Court of Honor on Wisconsin Avenue. Today the tradition is continued with the city tree placed in MacArthur Square each Yuletide.

1914   January. Milton Potter becomes school superintendent, a post he holds until the Second World War.

April. In the first Non-Partisan election,

Mayor Bading is re-elected, although Socialist Emil Seidel receives 43.5 per cent of the
votes. Hoan is easily re-elected attorney,
but charges that Bading restricted his campaign against the traction company and the
"Asphalt Ring." Hoan's suits maintain the
nickel fare, force the Railway Co. to pave
outside its track, and win riparian rights
for Milwaukee harbor improvements.

May 25. The first building code for Milwaukee passes the council.

August. World War One begins, and the Wisconsin German Alliance condemns the American
press as British oriented. The organization
raises funds by selling the Kaiser's portrait
to Milwaukee residents.

November 7. Wisconsin voters defeat greater
"home rule" privileges for Milwaukee.

November. The Mount Sinai Hospital opens
after the Jewish Community matches a $50,000
bequest from Abraham Slimmer.

1915   June 9. Hundreds of confiscated slot machines are destroyed by the city.

June 18. A memorial honoring Increase Lapham
is unveiled in Lapham Park.

The first Polish language theater in Milwaukee is opened.

1916   January. President Woodrow Wilson visits pro-
German Milwaukee and speaks in the Auditorium.

March. A bazaar raises $150,000 to relieve
German and Austrian war refugees.

April 4. Daniel Hoan is elected mayor of
Milwaukee with 33,863 votes, defeating Bading
(32,206). His council is composed of twenty-
six non-partisans and eleven Socialists.

April 19. Hoan signs a $750,000 act that ap-
proves the installation of a city-owned
street lighting system. Milwaukee's "sewer
socialism," however, never puts public utilities under municipal ownership.

May 13. Hoan leads 70,000 marchers in a

"Civic Demonstration," as Milwaukee refuses
to celebrate "Preparedness Day."

June. Milwaukee begins to install new street
lights.

The Ford Motor Company opens a $6,500,000
plant.

October. The Milwaukee _Journal_ begins to
editorialize against the pro-German stance
of the city, a campaign that wins a Pulitzer
Prize (June 2, 1919).

November. Milwaukee gives anti-war Wilson a
6,000-vote plurality.

December. Milwaukee completes the greatest
grain trade in its history; the city received 86,522,686 bushels, with most of it
used by the breweries.

1917   March 17. Seven thousand Milwaukee men rally
to assert their loyalty to America.

April 12. Although the Wisconsin Legislature
opposes war by 68-15, America declares hos-
tilities against Germany. The Deutscher Club
(in Alexander Mitchell's mansion) is trans-
formed into the Wisconsin Club, and the County Council of Defense is organized (April
30). The Pabst Theater suspends all German
plays, and the Chicago Symphony (which visits
Milwaukee each Monday) declines to perform
Brahms, Wagner, or Beethoven.

June 5. Milwaukee is the first large American city to complete its draft registration.
The city will vastly oversubscribe its quota in each of five "Liberty Loan" drives.

June 17. Milwaukee markets "war bread" whose
wheat content is reduced by one-fourth.

September 9. Bay View Italians riot against
the draft. However, 25,802 Milwaukee men
accept induction and 750 die in the conflict.

October 17. The anti-war _Milwaukee Leader_ is
denied second class mailing privileges.

November. The continuing opposition to the
draft leads to bombings. One "infernal de-

vice," discovered in the Italian Episcopal
church, explodes in a police station, killing
nine policemen and a woman.

December 10. The Milwaukee Association of
Commerce is organized.

1918   March. Hoan vetoes a council resolution
that provides for a city purchase of $500,000
in Liberty Bonds.

March 19. Hoan leads the primary field and
the voters abolish the thirty-seven man
council.

March 22. The Wisconsin Loyalty Legion is
founded to combat Socialism, pro-Germanism
and lack of Americanism.

April 2. Hoan is re-elected mayor, defeating
Percy Bremen 37,485 to 35,396. The voters
approve a council of twenty-five aldermen
serving four-year terms.

April. The German Theater suspends its
season.

August. The study of German is made optional
in elementary schools. By December only
400 students will take it, as opposed to
30,000 in 1916.

October. President Wilson signs a law that
prohibits the manufacture of intoxicating
beverages after May 1, 1919. Beer production
plummets this year to 2,217,000 barrels and
gloom pervades the 1,900 Milwaukee saloons.

November. Victor Berger, under indictment
along with four other Socialists for viola-
tion of the Espionage Act, is elected to
Congress from Milwaukee's 5th District. The
House refuses to seat him by a vote of 309-1.

December 9. Berger goes on trial before
Judge Keneshaw Mountain Landis.

December 23. The Linwood Avenue intake for
Lake Michigan water is completed.

December. Eleven hundred and eight deaths
are reported among Milwaukee's 18,000 cases
of Spanish influenza.

1919   January. Leo Stern, leader of the German
            American Alliance, is forced to resign as
            assistant superintendent of schools.

            January 18. An audience boos down Mayor
            Hoan during a ceremony honoring returning
            soldiers.

            February 20. After denying new trials to the
            Socialists, Judge Landis sentences them to
            five to twenty years in prison.

            June. The teaching of German in the elemen-
            tary schools is discontinued.

            July 1. The beginning of prohibition on the
            sale of liquor closes breweries and saloons
            and begins fourteen years, five months and
            five days of the "noble experiment." However,
            according to Mayor Hoan, "the whole U. S.
            Army couldn't dry up Milwaukee" and over
            3,000 Prohibition convictions in federal court
            tend to prove his point. The Schlitz Co.
            begins to manufacture Eline Candy Bars.

            August 28. Albert Lawson begins a 3,000-
            mile air promotional trip and is rewarded
            with the first U. S. air mail contract. The
            city soon opens its first public airport,
            Currie Field.

            September 20. Hoan refuses to greet King
            Albert of Belgium -- "To hell with the King,
            I am for the common man."

            December. In a special election, Berger is
            re-elected to the Congress, which again re-
            fuses to seat him.

            Milwaukee ranks as the fourth American manu-
            manufacturing city. The value of its indus-
            trial output has risen 158 per cent since
            1914. Hoan and businessmen begin to demand
            federal aid for a seaway to link Milwaukee
            with the Atlantic Ocean.

1920   With a population of 457,147 Milwaukee is the
            second most densely populated American city,
            having 18,083 people per square mile. Its
            black population has more than doubled in a
            decade, but totals only 2,249.

            April 6. Dan Hoan is re-elected (40,530) to

a four-year term, defeating Clifton Williams
(37,205), who urged citizens to "Vote for
Milwaukee" and against Socialism; a Non-
Partisan majority is returned to the council.
The voters also approve plans for a civic
center.

June 1. The five-man Board of Harbor Commissioners replaces the Harbor Commission;
it acts as a port authority.

July 28. As its last action, the Harbor Commission approves a plan for port development
drawn by H. McClellen Harding.

Mrs. Goldie Myerson quits her job in the
Public Library to emigrate to Palestine; as
Golda Meir, she later becomes Israel's
prime minister.

October 4. The council condemns the harbor
property of the Illinois Steel Co. and begins
implementation of the Harding Plan.

November 15. Milwaukee adopts a comprehen-
sive zoning plan.

1921   January 21. The Supreme Court reverses the
twenty-year conviction of Victor Berger.

May 7. Jacob Laubenheimer becomes chief of
police, a job he holds until 1936.

July. The Milwaukee Safety Commission is
created; among its innovations will be me-
chanical stop and go signals (1922), safety
islands (1923), and regulated parking (1925).
The three-man Metropolitan Sewerage Commission is also organized in 1921.

August. The Association of Commerce begins
to publish Milwaukee, a promotional trade
journal. The city this year acquires title
to Pabst Park (Garfield Park) and becomes
the first American city to sponsor low cost
cooperative public housing (Gardner Homes
project).

1922   April 26. Radio station WAAK opens in Gim-
bels department store.

September 22. Congress approves the Rivers
and Harbors Act which funds Outer Harbor

improvements.

November. Victor Berger is again elected to
congress and is seated at last; he wins reelection in 1924 and 1926.

Between 1922-29 Milwaukee negotiates forty-
seven annexations with its surrounding communities and adds fifteen square miles to
its territory. A real estate department is
created (1922) to plat the lands and chart
city development.

1924   January 1. The Public Debt Amortization Fund
Act requires Milwaukee to use one third of all
its interest to retire the public debt.

April 1. The Regional Planning Department
is organized.

April 5. Hoan (74,418) defeats David Rose
(57,495) and retains the mayoralty.

June 17. Public grain elevator "E" is destroyed by fire.

August. Heavy rains cause severe flooding
in several wards of the city.

George Devine opens the Wisconsin Roof, a
nightclub where Vaughan Monroe begins his
career.

November 4. The voters approve a home rule
amendment to the Wisconsin constitution which
permits the Milwaukee Charter to be amended
by simple council ordinance.

December. The police report an increase of
2500 per cent in drunken driving arrests
since 1919, and a total of 4,774 drunk arrests in 1924.

1925   Mayor Hoan names Peter J. Steinkellner fire
chief, and Dr. John Koehler health commissioner. They will help make Milwaukee the
safest city in America during the next fifteen
years.

June 24. The two square miles of Piggsville
are annexed.

June 26. The Jones Island Sewerage Plant

goes into operation. The milorganite produced by treatment is sold by the city, and
has since added well over $70,000,000 to
city revenues.

October 12. Hoan orders a halt to the tolling
of "Big Ben," city hall's eleven-ton bell,
because vibrations are weakening the building's foundation.

1927 The fire department is fully motorized by
Chief Steinkellner.

July 5. Regular air service to Chicago begins; air mail service has been in operation
since June 7, 1926.

1928 January 13. The "Milwaukee Road" emerges from
receivership as the Chicago, Milwaukee, St.
Paul and Pacific Railroad.

April. Hoan (64,874) defeats Charles Schal-
litz (46,657). He inaugurates a ten-year
program to upgrade city structures and raze
run-down buildings.

August 14. The city annexes another one-and-
a-half square miles.

September 12. The cornerstone of St. Mary's
College is dedicated.

November 18. Saint Josephat's is consecrated;
it became America's Polish Basilica by order
of Pope Pius IX on March 10, 1929.

1929 January 1. North Milwaukee is annexed. Milwaukee constructs 52.7 miles of street, 48.7
miles of water mains and 81.15 miles of storm
sewers to service its burgeoning population.

April 2. The Wisconsin voters repeal the
Severen Act and approve beer sales of not
more than 2.75 per cent alcohol by weight.

May. Dan Hoan, who had distributed surplus
food in the postwar depression of 1919, is
forced to pay a $6,000 judgment to the city
for using its equipment and employees to
run the project.

July 9. The Municipal Car Ferry Terminal
opens; it receives fifty-seven per cent of

Milwaukee's water commerce over the next
decade.

August 7. Victor Berger dies of injuries
after being struck by a Milwaukee streetcar.

October 1. Paul Block becomes owner and publisher of the Sentinel.

October 9. Fire partially destroys the Bell
Tower of city hall.

October 22. In the same month that the
Federal government completed a breakwater,
a storm destroys 500 feet of the wall, sinks
the car ferry Milwaukee and floods thousands
of homes.

December. Although the Depression has begun,
Milwaukee ranks as the second American city
in concentration of industry. It has won the
Intercity Health Contest of the National
Chamber of Commerce and has opened a new
airfield named after its greatest soldier,
General "Billy" Mitchell.

1930   January. Although the county has already
dispensed $600,000 in relief funds, fewer
than 1,000 Milwaukee families are on welfare.

June 2. Milwaukee elects the first woman
Presbyterian elder, Mrs. S. E. Dickson.

November. The Transients Service Bureau opens
in an armory -- a free kitchen is established
by Mayor Hoan to dispense food donated by
city merchants.

December. Milwaukee's 578,249 residents live
in a city of forty-one square miles. The
population is now only 18.9 per cent foreign
born, and forty-seven per cent of its families own their own homes. Black population
has tripled in a decade (7,501) and is con-
centrated in a twelve block area of the Sixth
Ward.

1931   March. The Milwaukee Securities Market is
organized.

May 1. Milwaukee is redistricted into twen-
ty-seven wards.

June 10. The Milwaukee Grain and Stock Exchange is created from members of the Chamber
of Commerce.

The city opens an $8,000,000 courthouse de-
signed by Albert Ross, a public library and
museum building designed by Ferry and Clas,
and an air-marine terminal.

1932   March 1. Milwaukee Communists condemn Hoan
for betraying the workers through cooperation with Capitalism.

April. Hoan (108,279) defeats Alderman J.
Carney (62,511) and remains mayor; Socialists
also elect the city treasurer and attorney.
With support from two independent candidates,
Hoan enjoys a council majority until 1936.

April 19. Hoan's inaugural predicts "world
wide economic and social revolution that
will not cease until. . . . capitalism is entirely replaced by . . .socialism."

June 10. West Allis riots against outdoor
relief procedures.

August 8. David Rose, five times Milwaukee's
mayor, dies.

September. When Franklin D. Roosevelt speaks
to the Milwaukee's Eagles, 200,000 citizens
turn out to greet him.

November 5. Pabst takes over the Premier
Malt Products Co. and soon becomes the first
brewery to introduce canned beer on a national basis.

December. Depression reduces Milwaukee employment to 66,010 while fifty per cent of
city property taxes are uncollected. The
city inaugurates a policy of refusing to issue general obligation bonds, and Mayor Hoan
proposes to pay city payrolls partially in
scrip.

1933   January. Hoan appoints the first city Housing
Commission and receives its report from Chairman Frank Harder in September.

February. Hoan serves as vice chairman of
the U. S. Conference of Mayors which demands

Federal urban relief.

March 29. Four thousand attend an anti-
Nazi meeting in Plankinton Hall, but George
Froboese still organizes a strong German-
American Bund in Milwaukee.

April 7. The legalization of 3.2 per cent
beer aids Milwaukee's recovery. Fifty thousand people mob the Schlitz factory in a
town where 140,000 people (twenty per cent
of the population) receive welfare.

December 5. Prohibition is repealed. By
year's end Milwaukee beer sales have ex-
ceeded $30,000,000.

December 19. The nation's first U.H.F. fac-
simile broadcast is made in Milwaukee.

1934   January. A fifteen-man commission is appointed to investigate consolidation of the
city and county of Milwaukee.

June. A tugboat strike divides Milwaukee
as all bridges are raised to allow ships to
negotiate the rivers without assistance. At
least 107 industrial conflicts punctuate the
year, the most tragic at the Electric Railway
and Light Co., where a man is accidentally
electrocuted (June 29).

July 20. A special Milwaukee Road train
breaks the world record for sustained high
speed by steam power. Ninety-minute service
to Chicago is instituted.

November 6. Milwaukee votes to allow officials to serve on both county and city governments, but consolidation is rejected by the
state legislature. Seventy-one city ordinances (since 1925) are incorporated into a revised city charter.

November 20. Hoan becomes president of the
U. S. Conference of Mayors.

Milwaukee is barred from further competition
in the National Health Conservation Contest
in order to give other cities a chance; its
death rate falls to eight per thousand. The
city is awarded the Grand Prize from the
National Safety Council.

1935   January 28. Fire causes $200,000 worth of
damage to St. John's Cathedral.

February 1. Lucius Nieman, editor of the
<u>Journal</u> for fifty-three years, dies.

September 30. The Boncel Law permits Hoan
to close struck plants if there is danger to
public safety.

November 3. Five midwestern <u>Bunds</u> meet in
Milwaukee to hear an address by Fritz Kuhn.

November 9. Idzi Rutkowski, the "Mad Bomber
of Milwaukee" is killed when his dynamite
cache explodes and before the city responds
to his ransom demands.

December. The P.W.A. financed addition to
the Jones Island Sewerage Plant is completed.

The Milwaukee Historical Society is incorporated.

1936   January. Milwaukee has negotiated ninety-
six annexations, sixty-one of them for less
than a quarter of a square mile, in its
ninety years as a municipality.

February 1. "Billy" Mitchell, advocate of
air power, dies.

February-August. The Newspaper Guild strikes
Hearst's <u>Wisconsin News</u> and wins both union
recognition and better wages.

April 7. Hoan (111,561) defeats Joseph
Shinners (98,897) but the Non-Partisans re-
gain council control and repeal the Boncel
Law. Voters approve the transfer of all
city parks to the county board and the two
systems merge on January 1, 1937.

April. The first oil tanker docks in Milwaukee.

July. The C.I.O. begins an organizational
drive in Milwaukee's industrial plants. At
the Allis-Chalmers Works 6,500 workers join
the union.

August 23. Police Chief Laubenheimer dies
and is replaced by a Socialist, Joseph Klu-

chesky.

December. Milwaukee has the lowest burglary
insurance rate and the lowest auto theft rate
of any large American city.

1937   April. The voters reject Hoan's advice and
            grant to the city council the right to fill
            vacancies.

            July. Seventy C.I.O. affiliated unions form
            the Industrial Union Council.

            September. Cardinal Strich College opens.

            December. Milwaukee has won the National
            Safety Contest for the fourth time and its
            victory in the National Health Award bars it
            from further competition. It also boasts
            the nation's lowest car death and homicide
            rates.

1938   August 24. The Blatz Temple of Music in Wash-
            ington Park is dedicated as "Music under the
            Stars" is inaugurated.

            September. Lucius Nieman Fellowships are
            established at Harvard.

            October. The Milwaukee Electric Railway
            and Light Co. becomes the Wisconsin Electric
            Company.

            December. Although fourth among all Great
            Lake ports, Milwaukee's water borne traffic
            has not expanded since 1920.

1939   July 2. Complete water filtration is a-
            chieved in Milwaukee when a new purification
            plant goes into operation.

            November 20. The city obtains a $546,124
            judgment against West Allis in a water rate
            case.

            December. Milwaukee wins first place in the
            National Traffic Safety Award Contest for the
            ninth successive year. It wins its fourth
            successive first in Public Health, and is
            ranked first in fire prevention.

THE MODERN CITY
1940-1976

1940   March 12. Hoan runs first in the primary
                election.

                April 2. Carl Zeidler (111,957) defeats
                Hoan (99,798) and becomes Milwaukee's second
                "Boy Mayor." His campaign consisted of anti-
                Socialist talks and innumerable renditions of
                "God Bless America."

                Wire mesh is installed around the inner well
                of city hall, the scene of eight suicides.

                December. A Citizen's Bureau report calls
                for additional harbor improvements as muni-
                cipal dock traffic has doubled in a year.
                Milwaukee, with a population of 587,472 is
                the thirteenth largest American city, and
                fourth in concentration of industry. Iron
                and steel continue to dominate its commerce,
                followed by leather products and food.

1941   January. The Selective Service reports that
                71,000 Milwaukee youths have registered for
                the draft.

                September 15-18. An American Legion Con-
                vention, lured to the city by Mayor Zeidler,
                convenes.

                The widening and repaving of Kilbourn Avenue
                is completed. Proposals to develop the Lake
                Front are approved by the Public Land Com-
                mission.

                December. For the first time in a decade,
                city land values increase.

1942   April 8. Mayor Zeidler accepts a commission
                in the Naval Reserve, and is replaced as
                mayor by John Bohn.

                April. The city halts support to the Art
                Institute.

                July 30. The City Council of Defense con-
                ducts a blackout.

                September 8. A staggered work hour plan is
                adopted to relieve traffic congestion.

December. Carl Zeidler is lost on the <u>La-Salle</u> somewhere off Africa.

1943   Summer. Two-way radio systems are installed
            for the police and fire departments and the
            city adopts a curfew to reduce juvenile
            delinquency.

            August 1. Five city taxing units adopt cost
            of living increase plans for their workers.

            November 3. Public Works Department employ-
            ees begin a month's strike.

            December. The comptroller reports that amor-
            tization funds exceed Milwaukee's debt by
            $10,000,000 -- the city is debt-free.

1944   April. John Bohn is elected mayor and cre-
            ates a commission on Human Rights.

            May 1. The Milwaukee Housing Authority is
            established. In the next twenty-five years,
            it finances $63,000,000 in public housing.

1945   April-June. All Milwaukee thrills to the
            saga of "Gertie the Duck," who laid her eggs
            on a piling in the Milwaukee River. Press
            coverage exceeds that for the end of the war
            in Europe.

            August. The war in the Pacific ends. Over
            500 Milwaukee men worked on, and seventy-
            seven Milwaukee plants produced parts for,
            the Atomic Bomb.

            December. Low income housing for the Sixth
            Ward is approved. A survey by the <u>Journal</u>
            indicates that Milwaukeans intend to leave
            the central city; Milwaukee is now surrounded
            by an "iron ring" of suburbs.

1947   January 29-30. Seventeen inches of snow halt
            all Milwaukee traffic.

            February 1. A master plan for city develop-
            ment is adopted.

            April. Milwaukee votes to modify its no-debt
            policy; "pay as you go" has resulted in cen-
            tral city deterioration and fewer major pro-
            jects.

November 9.   The Allis Art Library opens.

November 10.   The council adopts an integra-
ted Expressway plan. A system of one-way
streets also goes into effect this year.

December 3. WTMJ-TV, the eleventh station
in America, begins broadcasting.

The Milwaukee Journal begins thirteen years
as the world's leading newspaper in color
advertising.

1948   March.   Dan Hoan runs fourth in the non-partisan primary.

April 6.   Frank Zeidler (124,024) is elected
Milwaukee's third Socialist mayor, defeating
Henry Reuss (97.277).   The voters approve
$13,000,000 in bonded projects and effective-
ly end "pay as you go."   Zeidler will combat
the "iron ring" by doubling the area of Milwaukee in a decade.

The city sanitation department is completely
motorized. For the fifteenth consecutive
year, Milwaukee has the lowest traffic death
rate in America.

November.   The Mayor's Commission on Econom-
ics reports in favor of a no-debt policy although conceding "the city needs a face
lifting job."

December.   The first families move into Hill-
side Terrace, a low-rent housing project.
Three more projects open in 1949.   The Metropolitan Youth Commission is created to
deal with delinquency.

1950   City population reaches 637,392, ninety per
cent of whom are American born. Germans and
Poles dominate its ethnic base, while Catho-
licism remains the predominant religion.
All non-whites together compose only 3.6
per cent of the population.

1952   April.   Zeidler obtains 72.5 per cent of the
vote in winning re-election.

September 10.   The Milwaukee Journal begins
to editorialize against Senator Joseph Mc-
Carthy, although he is at the height of his

influence.

October 13. The Milwaukee and Suburban Transport Corporation purchases the city transportation system for $10,000,000.

December. The council approves an expressway
scheme that becomes the basis of all city
traffic flow patterns.

1953   March 18. The franchise of the Boston Braves
            Baseball Club is transferred to Milwaukee.

            April 7. Milwaukee votes in favor of fluori-
            dating its water supply.

            The Milwaukee Pops Orchestra is organized.

            May 14-July 28. Milwaukee brewery workers
            go out on strike in order to win contracts
            comparable to East and West Coast workers.
            The strike is won because the Blatz Brewery
            accepts their demands, but Blatz is ousted
            from the Brewers Association for "unethical"
            business methods.

            September. The Milwaukee Braves draw
            1,826,397 fans in their first year and set a
            National League attendance record.

            October. A $10,000,000 vocational school
            building is completed.

1954   January 1. Milwaukee redistricts itself into
            eighteen wards.

            April 6. The voters approve an $18,000,000
            school bond issue.

            April 7. The town of Lake is annexed and be-
            comes Milwaukee's nineteenth ward.

1956   April 3. Frank Zeidler is reelected mayor
            over Milton McGuire, winning 55.6 per cent
            of the vote; no other Socialist wins election.
            Both Milwaukee and the Town of Granville ap-
            prove consolidation, but legal suits delay
            annexation until 1962.

            August. President Dwight D. Eisenhower, un-
            der pressure led by Mayor Zeidler, vetoes a
            bill that would have allowed Chicago to di-
            vert Lake Michigan water to the Illinois

River.

September. The University of Wisconsin at
Milwaukee becomes operative, as the UW ex-
tension division merges with Milwaukee
State Teachers College.

November 6. The voters approve a $7,540,000
bond issue to aid the Museum, especially
its trans-Mississippi frontier collection.

1957   February 5. A broad program of urban renewal
is adopted by the council.

April 2. The largest bond issue in city history, $39,000,000 for school construction,
wins approval.

May. The _Journal_ runs a series on "The Negro
in Milwaukee."

July 20. Governor Vernon Thompson approves
the Metropolitan Study Commission to deal with
Milwaukee problems.

September 12-October 20. The New Art Center,
a merger of the Layton Gallery with the Art
Institute, opens with a showing of paintings
by El Greco, Rembrandt, Van Gogh, and Pi-
casso. The gallery is part of the War Memorial Center designed by Eero Saarinen.

October. Led by M.V.P. Hank Aaron, the Braves
win the National League pennant and the World
Series.

October-November. Three hundred thousand
cases of Asian Flu are reported in Milwaukee.

1958   October 1. The Milwaukee Redevelopment Authority is created.

October. The Braves repeat as NL Champions,
but lose the World Series to the New York
Yankees.

December. The port has a record 261 ocean
sailings. The Harbor Commission begins to
spend $11,000,000 on piers, access roads,
terminals and dredging in anticipation of the
opening of the St. Laurence Seaway.

1959   January 27. William Cousins is installed as

Milwaukee's Catholic archbishop.

June 26. The St. Laurence Seaway officially opens.

July 7. Queen Elizabeth II sails through the Outer Harbor on her way to Chicago. The U. S. Marines stage a mock landing on McKinley Beach to culminate the seaway festivities.

July. A $60,000,000 East Side renewal plan is announced by the Redevelopment Authority.

The Marine National Exchange Bank wins a long battle to obtain a tax abatement and begins to construct the twenty-eight story Marine Plaza, completed in 1962.

September 3. Zeidler presides over a conference on "inner core" problems; Councilmen attack him as a "nigger lover."

October 31. Zeidler announces he will not run for reelection due to his health. However, the industrial tax base has fallen $8,000,000 in a year and new leadership seems necessary.

December. Milwaukee reports 332 Seaway sailings; its overseas trade has doubled to 177,847 short tons. Ships from Israel, Switzerland, and Spain visit the port.

1960   April 5. Henry Maier defeats Henry Reuss by 35,000 votes and becomes the thirty-seventh mayor of Milwaukee. His problems include the "iron ring" and increasing racial tension in the core city.

April 13. Construction begins on a $14,000,000 addition to the Journal Building; a poll of 335 daily newspaper editors ranks that paper third in America, behind the New York Times and the Christian Science Monitor.

June. Utilizing academic advisors as counselors, Maier realigns all city departments into four "do" (development operation) units.

September. Construction of a new museum starts. The city has purchased the Pabst Theater and leases it to theater groups in order to assure continued operation.

December. With a population of 741,324 Milwaukee ranks as America's eleventh largest
city. It is the ninth greatest manufacturing
center in America ($3.5 billion) and it leads
the world in production of diesel and gas
engines, outboard motors, motorcycles, tractors, padlocks and beer. Its unemployment
rate is under three per cent, although the
rate is significantly higher among the
62,458 (8.9 per cent) blacks in the city.
However, its bonded debt has risen 1700 per
cent since 1950.

1961   April. A Wisconsin referendum obviates the
          need for jury trials in land condemnation and
          makes possible Milwaukee's urban renewal
          program.

          June 11. Daniel Hoan, mayor for twenty-four
          years, dies.

          July. Frank Lloyd Wright's "gem," the An-
          nunciation Greek Orthodox Church, is opened.

          July 31. The council approves Maier's De-
          partment of City Development, and on October
          5 Richard Perrin becomes its director.

          September. Municipal Pier #2 is completed.

          November 15-December 11. The _Journal_ suffers
          its first strike.

          December. Seaway tonnage triples in a year
          to 685,363 short tons; grain exports rise
          from 16,270 to 192,015 tons.

1962   April. Milwaukee purchases _The Seagull_, a
          ship with the capacity to remove floating
          debris from the harbor. The city also sends
          a trade mission to Europe. Congress author-
          izes dredging to a depth of twenty-seven
          feet, which enables the port to accomodate
          all seaway shipping.

          Summer. Some city beaches, closed since 1959
          due to water pollution, reopen.

          July 4. The city first adopts the "Circus
          World" theme that still highlights its "Old
          Milwaukee" Independence Day parade.

          July 19. The _Journal_ Company purchases the

Sentinel, whose publication had been halted
by a strike. The first edition of the new
paper is issued on July 23.

September 24. Maier's Social Development
Commission is created.

1963   Milwaukee organizes a "land bank" to acquire
land and make it available for industrial development. This bank, one of the few successful such operations in America, has enabled some twenty companies to relocate on
city sites in the central core, and has substantially improved the city's economy.

July. The first CORE chapter in Milwaukee
is formed.

December. Milwaukee boasts the nation's lowest crime rate, having fewest murders, rapes,
assaults, robberies, burglaries and auto
thefts in its population category.

1964   January. The city is redistricted into nineteen wards.

February. Harold Breier becomes police
chief and continues the "tough cop" tradition
of the department.

April 7. George Wallace, governor of Alabama, wins thirty-four per cent of Democratic
votes in the Wisconsin presidential primary.
He tells audiences that, if forced to leave
Alabama, "I'd want to live on the South Side
of Milwaukee."

Maier is reelected and advocates "The Milwaukee Idea" -- he serves as president of
the National League of Cities.

May 18. The Milwaukee United School Integration Committee (MUSIC) organized to protest _defacto_ school segregation, initiates
its first boycott.

December 16. President Lyndon Johnson announces the award of $312,565 to the Social
Development Commission.

1965   January. Milwaukee is selected as one of
eighteen cities to host a federal Youth Opportunity Center.

Spring. Three conservatory domes, housing tropical, temperate and desert flowers, open in Mitchell Park.

April. Construction of a new federal post office begins (completed 1968).

The city announces $112,000,000 in urban renewal projects, and the Public Museum opens a permanent exhibit on "The Streets of Old Milwaukee."

May-June. Superintendent of Schools Harold Vincent declares integration of the school system is "administratively unfeasible."

August. The Amtrack Corporation opens one of the few new railroad terminals in America.

October 18-21. Father James E. Groppi leads a three-day boycott against de facto segregation of schools. Maier orders a study on why the white majority has a distorted image of the city's 90,000 blacks.

1966   January 28. After ten years of success, the franchise of the Milwaukee Braves is shifted to Atlanta, where the owners hope to tap an unexploited television market.

February 10. The Journal reports that blacks most resent the Milwaukee housing situation and, despite the school controversy, believe that more jobs will most benefit their community.

June 29. Maier launches the "Crusade for Resources" to demand tax redistribution and an easing of Wisconsin property taxes. By 1972, he leads a coalition of about 1,500 communities demanding tax reform.

1967   January 31. A study funded by Milwaukee presents plans for a "War against Prejudice."

May 1. The Milwaukee Journal is awarded a Meritorious Public Service Pulitzer Prize for its campaign against water pollution.

July 30-31. Riots, participated in by some 300 blacks, grip Milwaukee: three die, 100 are injured (including forty-four policemen) and 1,740 people are arrested.

August 6. Archbishop William Cousins demands
an end to Catholic prejudice, defends the
right of clergy to protest discrimination,
and creates the Council on Urban life to
deal with inner city issues.

August 28. Father Groppi begins a series of
demonstrations for open housing that will
last 200 days. He will ultimately lead his
demonstrators across the "longest bridge in
the world" -- the one between Poland and Africa -- which connects the East and South
Sides of Milwaukee.

September. The U. S. Commission on Civil
Rights reports that eighty-seven per cent of
Milwaukee blacks attend segregated schools.

September 7. Sit-in demonstrators destroy
Maier's office.

October. Maier and the city council table
open housing legislation.

December 12. Milwaukee's council enacts a
carbon copy of Wisconsin's State Housing Law.

1968   February 9. Father Groppi is convicted of
resisting arrest, is fined $500, and given
two years probation.

April 2. Maier crushes David Walther and is
reelected with eighty-six per cent of the
vote. He coins the phrase "reorder national
priorities."

The Midtown Conservation Project begins to
re-house persons displaced by renewal.

April 8. Fifteen thousand silent and non-
violent marchers honor the memory of Martin
Luther King.

April 30. Maier leads the council in passing
an open housing law that is stronger than the
federal model.

July. The nine-day _Sumerfest_ is inaugurated,
and over 1,250,000 attend.

1969   May 22. Milwaukee applies to H.U.D. for
Model City aid.

June 21-August 10. The Milwaukee Art Center
and the Schlitz Co. sponsor an art exposition, "Aspects of the New Realism."

August. Only six per cent of the voters turn
out to vote for Neighborhood Resident Council
boards. Maier candidates defeat those of
the largely black Organization of Organizations (Triple O), and he retains the leadership of Milwaukee's Model Cities Program.

September 17. The $12,000,000 Performing
Arts Center opens. Its showpiece, Uihlein
Hall, becomes home to the Milwaukee Sym-
phony Orchestra (organized 1959).

October 3. Israeli Premier Golda Meir visits
her hometown.

December. Milwaukee is honored in 1969 as
"Beautiful City -- U.S.A." and wins the
Trigg Trophy in the National "Clean Up, Paint
Up, Fix Up" competition. Crime rates fall
fourteen per cent (despite a national rise of
eleven per cent) and, since 1964, the city
boasts the best traffic safety record in
America.

1970   March 31. Major league basebal returns to
Milwaukee as the American League Brewers
arrive.

April 10. Father Groppi resigns his parish
duties. He marries in 1976 and is excommu-
nicated.

Summer. About 45,000 residents petition the
council to freeze property tax rates at 1969
levels.

Milwaukee completes its 157th school.

The Moon Rock display at the Public Museum
is attended by 129,778 citizens.

September 25. A "have not" conference hears
gubernatorial candidates of both parties
praise tax relief. Henry Maier, who has e-
normously increased the power of his office
since 1960, leads the campaign that elects
Patrick Lucey.

December. Milwaukee is America's twelfth
largest city, with a population of 717,372

(16.3 per cent minorities). However, since 1960 the city has lost 70,200 whites in the "flight to the suburbs." Milwaukee remains world leader in the production of gasoline and diesel engines, electrical equipment, and beer. Completed harbor improvements enable the port to handle 6,000,000 tons of freight and, for the first time, it exports 1,000,000 tons of foreign trade.

1971   January. The bureaus of Street Sanitation and Garbage Collection merge as the city has contracted for private refuse service.

February. The "blue flu" strikes the police department; strikers claim arbitration victory in November.

May. The Milwaukee Bucks win the National Basketball Championship.

June. Maier is elected president of the U.S. Conference of Mayors. Its Legislative Action Committee visits Milwaukee to call for action on the urban crisis (July 19-22).

August 7. Maier attacks Milwaukee County encroachments on city-owned property. He begins a program of scattering low-income housing throughout the city and HUD promises greater federal support if Milwaukee eliminates restrictive building codes.

August 14. The American Indian Movement (AIM) seizes an abandoned Coast Guard Station and converts it into an alcoholic treatment center.

September 25. Milwaukee Model Cities is mocked by South Siders; they create a "Model Alley" and send construction bills to the city.

December. Wisconsin grants Milwaukee tax relief of $11,500,000.

December 18. Maier denounces the city coverage of both the _Journal_ and the _Sentinel_.

1972   Kenneth Fry, director of City Development, resigns.

March-June. The port of Milwaukee is closed

by a longshoremen's strike.

April. Maier is again elected mayor; he
won sixty-seven per cent of the vote in his
race with Bernard Nowak, despite repudiating
the editorial support of the _Journal_. Construction on a convention center and a harbor
bridge reduces unemployment to six per cent,
and Maier's major concern is public anger
against freeway construction.

May 27. Police Chief Breier says the force
lacks enough blacks -- this is after the fa-
tal shooting of a black woman by a white
detective.

August. Mrs. Henry Maier seconds the nomi-
nation of Richard Nixon.

1973   January 4-10. Eleven thousand public employees strike. A March settlement gives
them a six per cent raise.

January 31. Two white policemen are killed
by a black. Before he is caught and convicted, Milwaukee's black community reacts a-
gainst police tactics and charges harassment.

March 30. R. C. Nowakowski, chairman of the
county board, is indicted on felony charges.
He will be found guilty of bribery in February, 1974.

October 6. The $50,000,000 First Wisconsin
Center (42 floors, 601 feet high, designed
by Skidmore, Owings and Merrill) is dedicated. Milwaukee's $14,000,000 Convention
Center (designed by Nelson Becket) also
opens.

November 8. After "red Flu" strikes the fire
department, Maier declares a state of emer-
gency. National Guard mobilization forces
arbitration of the dispute.

1974   September-October. Washington High School is
swept by racial tension, a situation com-
pounded when the American Nazi Party attempts
to recruit new members.

December. A recall campaign against the
board that increased school taxes by twenty-
six per cent raises over 7,000 signatures.

1975   February 4. A school strike is settled.

            April 21. The _Journal_ wins the Scripps-
            Howard Foundation Award.

            May. Milwaukee's ratio of city debt service
            to the current budget is a very dangerous
            15.2 per cent, but Maier declares most city
            problems are due to white flight.

            August 25. President Gerald Ford visits Mil-
            waukee and is interviewed on local televi-
            sion.

            September. The school board, for the first
            time, condemns racial segregation.

            December. A special Federal Census shows
            Milwaukee's population has fallen to 669,022
            with eighteen per cent of it black. Milwau-
            kee has eighty per cent of all Wisconsin
            blacks, its school system is thirty-five
            per cent black and it has lost an additional
            65,000 white residents since 1970.

1976   January 19. Federal Judge John Reynolds
            rules the Milwaukee School System is segre-
            gated.

            April. Maier is again elected mayor.

            Gerald Ford is in Milwaukee to campaign for
            the presidency, and his April 2, speech
            condemns Ronald Reagan's foreign policy.

            July 7. Judge Reynolds approves a three-
            year desegregation plan. By September, 66
            of 158 schools are to be twenty-five to
            forty-five per cent black.

            September 30. The American Geographical So-
            ciety of New York announces plans to relocate
            in Milwaukee.

            November 16. For the first time in four gen-
            erations, someone other than a Uihlein heads
            Schlitz as Daniel McKeithan is named Chairman.

1977   January 11. Milwaukee is charged with turn-
            ing Lake Michigan into a "giant toilet" by
            its dumping of raw sewage.

DOCUMENTS

The history of the City of Milwaukee is a near
classic case of American city development. Admirably
located at the confluence of three rivers, the site
possessed a vast hinterland while Lake Michigan provided
a route for Milwaukee to transport its resources to the
world. Milwaukee was successively a fur trading post,
a rough frontier village, a boom town, a commercial em-
porium and finally, a manufacturing center suffering
from urban blight. Always it ranked as the metropolis
of Wisconsin. The city's political history has been as
varied as its economic fortunes, with both sinners and
saints prominent in its annals. A city that welcomed
many foreign elements, it is almost invariably remembered
today as the first great American city to consistently
elect Socialists to positions of power. Yet today modern
Milwaukee is one of the most American of cities and
boasts an enviable record of stability, safety and security. The documents that follow chronicle the growth
of a metropolis that patiently endures the problems of
our times. Neither racial animosity nor the "iron ring"
of suburbs that surround them have swayed Milwaukeeans
from the conviction that their way of doing things is
best. Milwaukee continues to believe in <u>Gemutlichkeit</u>,
the good life, with such confidence that it always plea-
ses its visitors and can only amaze the historian.

MORGAN L. MARTIN DESCRIBES THE JUNEAU TRADING POST
1833

> Morgan L. Martin was a hard-headed
> Green Bay land speculator who in-
> tuitively recognized the potential
> of Milwaukee's location. After vi-
> siting the site in 1833, he quickly
> concluded a deal with fur trader
> Solomon Juneau to develop the area.
> Their partnership, cemented only
> by a handshake, guaranteed the de-
> velopment of Milwaukee.

Reuben Thwaites (ed.), "The Narrative of Morgan L. Martin," Collections of the State Historical Society of
Wisconsin, XI, 1888, 404-407.

I first visited Wisconsin in July, 1833, on a tour
of exploration. With me, were Daniel Le Roy and P. B.
Grignon, and we were mounted on horses. As far as
Fond du Lac, our course lay on the same trail that Judge
Doty and I had made in 1829. After that, we struck south-
east to the shore of Lake Michigan, following it closely
until the Milwaukee river was reached. Jacques Vieau
and Solomon Juneau traded at this point. I had known
them and their families since 1827, for their homes were
really in Green Bay, at which place they obtained all
their supplies. Both Vieau, senior, and Juneau were in
Chicago with the greater part of their families at the
time of our arrival: but young Jacques Vieau, son of the
elder, officiated under the parental roof.
When we set out on our tour, we agreed to eat everything we saw, and one time were compelled to thus dis-
pose of a hawk. At Milwaukee, there were no provisions
for us; but there were several Indians loafing around
and we engaged one of them to go out and get us some
ducks. These, Jacques cooked for us, and we ate them
cold upon our return trip, which was made by the way of
the lake shore. . . .
Both Solomon Juneau and Jacques Vieau were intelligent and worthy men, Mr. Juneau having the polished manners and airs of the French gentleman. In a certain History of Milwaukee, the latter has been described as being on a par with the Indians, as to intelligence and
manners. That they and their families were far removed
above the savage tribes by which they were surrounded, is
proven by the fact that they were enabled to procure
goods and supplies to a large amount on the usual credit
from the American Fur Company. Neither of them did at
that time regard themselves as permanent settlers of Mil-

waukee: but were temporary residents there for purposes
of trade with the Indians.   Their homes were in Green
Bay.   When I first visited Milwaukee in the summer of
1833, on the tour of exploration before narrated they
and their families were not there, the premises being in
charge of employees and one of Vieau's sons.   A further
evidence that all were mere sojourners was found in the
fact that no land was cleared, fenced, or even under cultivation, except a small patch of ground used by a bro-
ther of Juneau, in which he cultivated a few vegetables.
Subsequent events, however, proved Solomon Juneau to be
the first permanent settler, when the land he occupied
was ceded by the Indians and subjected to sale as government land.

From 1833 forward, I was a frequent and always welcome visitor to the house of Solomon Juneau. . . .

As a man, Solomon Juneau needs no encomiums from me.
He was always the same unselfish, confiding, open-hearted,
genial, honest and polite gentleman.   Our business relations commenced in October, 1833, and continued for several years.   His first hint of the prospective value of
his location at Milwaukee came from me, and he was so in-
credulous that it was sometimes difficult to prevent his
sacrificing his interest to the sharks who soon gathered
around him.   Himself the sour of honor, and unaccustomed
to the wiles of speculators, without a friend to caution
him he would have been an easy prey of designing individ-
uals. . . .

Juneau and I were joint owners of the original plat
of Milwaukee.   We never made any written memorandum of the
terms of our partnership and on account of his residence
on the spot he took the principal management of our joint
interest for more than three years.   At the close accounts
between us were adjusted and property valued at hundreds
of thousands divided, with as little difficulty as you
would settle a trifling store bill.

It would take a volume to enumerate the many admira-
ble traits of character which distinguished my late
friend, Solomon Juneau.   The intimate relations existing
between us made me well acquainted with his family, and
their everyday social relations.   Mrs. Juneau, instead of
the pure French of her husband, had a slight tincture of
Indian blood.   Her native tongue was French, and that
language was used in their family intercourse, though both
spoke English.   They probably had also acquired a knowledge of the languages of several Indian tribes, with
whom Mr. Juneau was accustomed to do business: but that
they "dressed and ate like Indians, and in their domestic
conversation spoke in the Indian tongue," is far from the
truth.   Mrs. Juneau was a most amiable and excellent woman, and many of the first settlers around Milwaukee will
no doubt bear ample testimony to the deeds of charity by
which she was distinguished.

NATHANIEL HYER RECALLS FRONTIER MILWAUKEE
1836

> The Morgan-Juneau partnership proved
> fruitful and Milwaukee grew rapidly.
> Prominent among the early settlers
> were not only traders and farmers,
> but also professional men like Na-
> thaniel F. Hyer, a lawyer who in
> 1880 recorded his impressions of a
> town "so evanescent" that he called
> it a "kaleidescope." Hyer's narra-
> tive graphically, but matter-of-
> factly, illustrated the harsh con-
> ditions of frontier life.

Source: <u>History of Milwaukee</u>, Chicago: Western Historical Co., 1881, 159-162.

I arrived in Milwaukee early in the month of May,
1836, from the steamer "New York." At that time the
courts had not been even rudely organized. Being a law-
yer, this was almost the first thing I learned. My fel-
low-passengers on the steamer, like myself and most of
those who had arrived before us, were too eager to find
or make a home in Wisconsin, then a part of Michigan
Territory. But little was cared for the illustration or
enforcement of other than the laws of necessity. We
landed at the mouth of the river, making shore in small
boats. After our luggage was stored in Chase's warehouse,
at the mouth of the river, many of us made our way on
foot along the narrow strip of dry land--situated on the
lake shore on the right and the impassable wet marsh on
the left--until we reached the bluff, which we followed
until we reached the dwelling of Solomon Juneau, near
the left bank of the Milwaukee River. The first thing
of note which we observed was a large number of small
white flags on stakes planted in the ground, which, we
were told, were to designate Indian graves. These could
be seen over all parts of the bluff along which we had
been walking. The savages deemed these signals would
protect the sacredness of their burial place from the
encroachments of Shumo-Kee man. . . .
A short distance from Juneau's house stood his store,
used as warehouse and post-office, which was crowded once
a day with a large part of the population, anxiously
waiting the delivery of the mail, which was delivered by
the assistant postmaster standing on a barrel and reading
in a loud voice the names of the happy receivers. When
all had been called the greater number retired with dis-
appointment. In looking about to find a resting place

for the night, I counted all the buildings in the town,
and found but forty roofs, all told. I finally procured
lodgings for a few days at Leland's, on the west side of
the river, and soon after a room in an unfinished building also on the West Side, where I unpacked my baggage
and put out my shingle. "Attorney-at-Law and Land Sur-
veyor." The latter profession I soon found to be most in
demand. The first surveying job presenting itself was
the laying out of Saukville, in the present County of
Washington. Here had been an Indian town of note. The
Indians had not all left the place, but were quite inof-
fensive, and the only call I had from them was for nails
to make a coffin for one of their dead. The next jobs
were laying out additions to the City of Milwaukee, and
the following Winter was engaged in staking out lots in
the tamarack swamp and wet marsh between the high bluff
and west bank of the river, which work could only be
done when the marsh was frozen.

At a mass meeting called at the suggestion of Governor Henry Dodge to nominate persons for the offices to be
filled by him under the first organization of the Territory of Wisconsin, which took effect July 4, 1836, I was
present, taking part in the proceedings. I was finally
nominated and later the Governor confirmed the choice in
issuing a commission. Daniel Wells, Jr., was nominated
at the same time for Justice of the Peace, and the Governor also issued a commission to him. I held court in
my office, which served me also as dormitory, the table
being my bedstead and some law books my pillow. Thus
was the "majesty of the law" first introduced into the
embryo City of Milwaukee, my jurisdiction extending over
the entire southeastern portion of Wisconsin.

On the 28th of September, 1836, a caucus was held to
fix upon a place and time for holding a mass meeting to
nominate delegates to the general convention to be held
"at Godfrey's." Godfrey's was a place of which no one
had any knowledge, except that it was on the Fox River,
in a south-westerly direction from Milwaukee; and that on
the map was a line called :"the trail to Godfrey's." The
mass meeting was held, at which, after much excitement,
the East Side and Walker's Point combined to beat the
West Side. They succeeded, and chose their nine delegates. The West Side then withdrew and chose nine other
delegates to represent their interests, and on the last
day of September, 1836, the double delegation started for
Godfrey's. I cannot recollect the names of all who went,
but know that Byron Kilbourn and his followers--of whom I
was one--led one side, and Alanson Sweet and his followers
led the other side. We were well prepared for the jour-
ney--in fact I may say that no body of delegates ever
travelled to a convention in such a manner, or under such
circumstances as that one. We started out equipped with
tents and camp furniture, such as blankets, provisions,

a "small" jug of comfort and each a knife and tin cup.
The cavalcade follwed the narrow trail very well, always
halting for me to go ahead over bad places, my remark
having been, on setting out, that the pony I was riding
could go where other ponies had gone. At nightfall we
had arrived in the midst of a large Indian corn-field,
the ears of which had been recently gathered. The trail
was lost; but after diligent search a path was found
which led into a stream of water about twenty feet in
width and of too great depth to ford. There was no al-
ternative--we must camp here for the night. We staked
out our ponies, pitched the tents, and prepared a supper.
This meal of victuals, however it might have appeared,
tasted good, Supper was soon dispatched; table cleared
and table-cloth shaken--which means that each arose and
brushed the cumbs from his own lap. We were then prepared for story-telling, and many a long yarn was spun
before the camp turned in for the night. At length bed-
time came and with it thirst--a desire for something more
cooling and soothing than the contents of the flasks which
had started out well-filled, to be used, doubtless, in
case of snake bite. There was no water near and no bucket
in which to fetch it. I soon improvised two buckets, however, by tying strings tightly around the legs of my
rubber overalls. With these novel water-pots I went to
a spring and brought a quantity of pure, cold water to
the camp, setting it near my tent door. With a curious
expression on his face, Byron Kilbourn enquired if it was
"expected that the delegates would drink our of my old
pantaloons." I replied that the water had been brought
for my own use, but all who desired could partake of it
and welcome. Kilbourn immediately quenched his thirst,
and before morning every one in the camp had drunk from
N. F. Hyer's "old pantaloons."

Early next morning we proceeded on our way, swimming
the creek, which all crossed in safety, though many were
in pretty damp clothing. After riding three or four miles
in this condition we arrived at Godfrey's, where a multi-
tude had already collected. The place consisted of one
log house of two rooms, which being more than full compelled us to take extra rooms on the open prairie, where
we again pitched our tents. After a hasty plate of soup
(which we failed to get,) we proceeded to hold the first
and most important political convention ever held in the
southeastern part of Wisconsin--including all the territory lying south of Brown and east of Iowa Counties. After much contention, the delegates first nominated at
Milwaukee were admitted, Alanson Sweet and Capt. Gilbert
Knapp were nominated and selected as the two counsellors
allowed to Milwaukee. . . . .

HARRIET MARTINEAU VISITS MILWAUKEE
1836

Despite all hardships Milwaukee
became a bustling village. Con-
fident pioneers sought fortunes
from the wilderness, while curious travelers, among them the
indefatigable Harriet Martineau,
made certain to stop at the boom
town. On her short visit to the
city she was impressed by its vi-
gor and beauty, but she noted its
difficult harbor.

Source: Harriet Martineau, Society in America, II,
London, 1837, 4-7.

A little schooner which left Chicago at the same
time with ourselves, and reached Milwaukee first, was a
pretty object. On the 29th, we were only twenty-five
miles from the settlement; but the wind was so unfavour-
anle that it was doubted whether we should reach it that
day. Some of the passengers amused themselves by gaming,
down in the hold; others by parodying a methodist sermon,
and singing a mock hymn. We did not get rid of them till
noon on the 30th when we had the pleasure of seeing our
ship disgorge twenty-five into one boat and two into another. The atmosphere was so transparent as to make the
whole scene appear as if viewed through an opera-glass;
the still green waters, the dark boats with their busy
oars, the moving passengers, and the struggles of one to
recover his had, which had fallen overboard. We were
yet five miles from Milwaukee; but we could see the
bright wooded coast, with a few white dots of houses.
While Dr. F. went on shore, to see what was to be
seen, we had the cabin cleaned out, and took, once more,
complete possession of it, for both day and night. As
soon as this was done, seven young women came down the
companion-way, seated themselves round the cabin, and began to question us. They were the total female population of Milwaukee; which settlement now contains four
hundred souls. We were glad to see these ladies; for it
was natural enough that the seven women should wish to behold two more, when such a chance offered. A gentleman
of the place, who came on board this afternoon, told me
that a printing-press had arrived a few hours before; and
that a newspaper would speedily appear. He was kind e-
nough to forward the first number to me a few weeks after-
wards; and I was amused to see how pathetic an appeal to
the ladies of more thickly-settled districts it con-

tained; imploring them to cast a favourable eye on Milwaukee, and its hundreds of bachelors. Milwaukee had
been settled since the preceding November. It had good
stores; (to judge by the nature and quantity of goods
sent ashore from our ship;) it had a printing-press and
newspaper, before the settlers had had time to get wives.
I heard these new settlements sometimes called "patri-
archal:" but what would the patriarchs have said to such
an order of affairs?

Dr. F. returned from the town, with apple-pies,
cheese, and ale, wherewith to vary our ship diet. With
him arrived such a number of towns-people, that the steward wanted to turn us out of our cabin once more: but we
were sturdy, appealed to the captain, and were confirmed
in possession. From this time, began the delights of
our voyage. The moon, with her long train of glory, was
magnificent to-night; the vast body of waters on which
she shone being as calm as if the winds were dead.

The navigation of these lakes is, at present, a mys-
tery. They have not yet been properly surveyed. Our
captain had gone to and fro on Lake Huron, but had never
before been on Lake Michigan; and this was rather an
anxious voyage to him. We had got aground on the sand-
bar before Milwaukee harbour; and on the 1st of July, all
hands were busy in unshipping the cargo, to lighten the
vessel, instead of carrying her up to the town. An ele-
gant little schooner was riding at anchor near us; and
we were well amused in admiring her, and in watching the
bustle on deck, till some New-England youths, and our
Milwaukee acquaintance, brought us, from the shore, two
newspapers, some pebbles, flowers, and a pitcher of fine
strawberries. . . .

While we were watching the red sunset over the leaden
waters, betokening a change of weather, the steamer "New
York" came ploughing the bay, three weeks after her time;
such is the uncertainty in the navigation of these stormy
lakes. She got aground on the sand-bank, as we had done;
and boats were going from her to the shore and back, as
long as we could see.

The next day there was rain and some wind. The captain and steward went off to make final purchases: but
the fresh meat which had been bespoken for us had been
bought up by somebody else; and no milk was to be had;
only two cows being visible in all the place.

RUFUS KING DESCRIBES A CITY IN THE WILDERNESS
1845

> In only a few years Milwaukee
> changed radically. When reporter
> Rufus King visited the town in
> 1845 he was overwhelmed, so much
> so that he left New York, where
> his family had long been prominent,
> and moved west. For the next twen-
> ty years he ranked as one of Mil-
> waukee's leading citizens.

Source: "Letters from the West," <u>Albany Evening Journal</u>,
June 30, 1845.

   I was prepared for a surprise on landing at Milwaukie, but what I actually saw far outran my expectations.
The approach of the boat was the signal for the assemb-
ling of some dozens of runners from the different Hotels
at the outer end of the pier, and when I had worked my
way through these I found myself in a maze of carts,
hackney coaches and omnibusses. Within a few minutes after landing, however, I made the acquaintance of Mr.
FILLMORE, the proprietor of the Milwaukie Sentinel, and
under his auspices was speedily installed in most comfortable quarters at the AMERICAN. I took the next day
to look round the town, and have been reflecting for two
or three days since whether people at the East will believe my "plain, unvarnished tale" of what Milwaukie <u>is</u>
when they remember that only ten years ago Milwaukie <u>was
not</u>. In 1835 the only inhabitant of the quarter section
which now constitutes the principal part of Milwaukie was
Mr. JUNEAU, an Indian trader. Now upon the same ground
stands a town of some EIGHT THOUSAND inhabitants, and
every steamboat, sailing vessel or propeller which comes
up the Lakes, brings constant accessions to this number.
The greatest part of this influx of population, too, has
taken place within five years back. Previous to 1840,
the growth of Milwaukie was quite slow. But in the latter year it took a sudden start, and has gone on since
steadily and rapidly increasing in size, substance and
population.
   MILWAUKIE is most advantageously situated -- From a
point about a mile or two to the North, the shore of the
Lake tends to the West, and sweeping gradually round,
forms a deep and wide bay. The Milwaukie River, swollen
by the waters of the Menominee, flows into the Lake near
the centre of the Bay. Between and on either side of the
two streams, spreads a broad flat, originally low and
wet, but now rapidly filling up, under the intelligent

enterprise of the Milwaukie people, with sand from the
river and gravel from the adjoining hills, the two together forming the best possible soil for a city plot.
The flat extends back rather more than a mile from the
Lake, and is from 1 to 2 miles in width, and it is en-
closed on all sides, except, of course, the water front,
by a belt of table-land, some fifty feet or more above
the level of the Lake, which is well timbered, and affords
numerous and beautiful sites for private residences.
Thus, it will be seen, if my description is intelligible,
that while the flat formed by the alluvial deposites of
the Milwaukie and Menomirее rivers furnishes a spacious
area for the business part of this growing town, the
table-land which surrounds it like the walls of an am-
phitheatre affords "ample room and verge enough" for
thousands of delightfully situated public or private
edifices.

I have said that Milwaukie already counts a population of eight thousand souls. It contains eleven churches
or meeting-houses.--2 Methodist, 1 Baptist, 1 Episcopal-
ian, 1 Presbyterian, 1 Congregational, 1 Unitarian, 1
Lutheran, 1 Catholic, and two others the denominations
of which I did not learn. Two more churches, one for
the Catholics, which is to cost seventy thousand dollars,
and one for the Baptists, have been commenced. Law
flourishes here as, strange to say, it seems to do in most
newly settled towns. I think the profession in Milwaukie
numbers forty-two-or-three members. There are eighteen
doctors, but the salubrity of the climate is such that
about one-half of them are without patients. A large
number of substantial and well filled stores line the
two or three principal streets, and several of the merchants, for the last two years, have done a retail business to the amount of forty or fifty thousand dollars.
There are three first-rate and about a score of second-
rate Hotels here. The former class includes the Milwaukie House, the City Hotel, and the American. I found
excellent quarters, and the most obliging of landlords,
at the latter. It is kept by Messrs. LOCKE & DARWIN, and
during the whole of my stay at Milwaukie was constantly
crowded. Such was the case, too, with the Milwaukie
House and the City Hotel, and, I presume, with the other
public houses, for the tide of travel through this place
is marvellous to behold -- The press is well represented
at Milwaukie. The Milwaukie Courier, a neatly-printed
and well conducted weekly paper, upholds the principles of
the Loco Focos, while the Milwaukie Sentinel, published
daily, as well as weekly, and edited with equal industry and
ability, by Messrs. JASON DOWNER and J. S. FILLMORE, is a
zealous and efficient champion of the Whig creed.

Many of the churches, stores and other buildings in
Milwaukee are of brick, and the bricks are made here.
They are of a light salmon color and, I should judge, but

little, if at all inferior, to the best of our Albany
bricks. Milwaukie river furnishes an abundant and reli-
able water-power. The river, which is about 300 feet in
width by from 10 to 14 in depth, is dammed a mile or
more above the town and the water for milling and factory
purposes is drawn off through a fine canal. A fall of
fourteen feet can be obtained, but ten is all' that is
used or needed at present. There is a large grist mill,
with four run of stone, a saw mill, two furnaces, a plan-
ing machine, a wooden ware factory, which turns out three
hundred pails, churns and tubs per day, and one or two
other establishments. The factories are all built between
the river and the canal. From the latter they derive
their supply of water and the former enables vessels of
all sizes to come up and moor immediately alongside. The
river runs through the heart of the town, and is spanned
by several drawbridges. The ware-houses, several of
which are of the largest class and most substantially
built, stand close upon the water's edge, so that vessels
can load and unload with dispatch and convenience.

There seems to have been some want of judgment in
the improvements which the General Government has made at
Milwaukie. The river, where it passes through the town,
runs a pretty strait course and so continues until within
a few rods of the Lake, where it makes a sudden sweep to
the south, winds along for a mile or more, nearly parallel
to the shore, and finally turns into the Lake. If the
beach had been cut through at the first bend (and some
years since the river discharged itself into the Lake
at this point) vessels coming into Milwaukie would have
been enabled to lay a strait course from the mouth of the
river up into the heart of the town. But instead of doing this, piers have been built out a thousand or twelve
hundred feet into the Lake at the present mouth of the
river, and a mile or two from the business part of the
town. Sailing vessels are frequently baffled by head
winds in this circuitous channel. The distance, too, of
the Government piers from the town is so considerable
that piers have been built by a company a mile nearer,
and within these most of the steamers and propellers
land. The number of emigrants and travellers of all sorts
who land at Milwaukie well nigh passes belief. During
the three days that I have been here, the average has
been two hundred a day, and for the last eight weeks the
average I am assured has been 15,000 per week. Many too
land at Racine and Southport. . . . But the great mass
of travel and immigration comes into the Territory through
Milwaukie, which is destined to be the chief commercial
and manufacturing city of this Western EMPIRE.

THE BRIDGE WAR
1845

Before Milwaukee could begin to
fulfill its destiny, however, it
had to settle the competition between the villages on opposite
sides of the Milwaukee River. Not
until the "Bridge War" of 1845 did
these rival developers realize the
futility of conflict and warily a-
gree to cooperate.

Source: This account of the war's origins is condensed
from Andrew C. Wheeler, The Chronicles of Milwaukee,
Milwaukee: Jermain & Brightman, 1861, 142-177.

It is curious to note the playful animosity which
had all along characterised the sections now becoming
tinctured with a bitterness that sprung from facied injuries received.
Certain of those on the west-side, had all along
proclaimed that the east-side was unhealthy; that foul
miasms hung over the houses; that the inhabitants lived
on frogs, which the Frenchman had learned them to eat,
and that many of them died and were buried at night, so
that the world should not see their depletion. The east-
siders had retaliated by calling them "country people,"
who had to cross the river to get into town; who had
no court house, no jail, "no nothing," but Byron Kilbourn.
One enthusiastic partizan had gone so far indeed as to
propose the establishment of a quarantine at the point
where the west-siders crossed the river. . . .
The first bridge had been built, in 1839, at Chestnut Street, and in 1843 Mr. Rogers, Pettibone and others,
constructed a floating bridge or raft at Spring Street.
This was carried away by a freshet, and a substantial
bridge was built in the spring of '43, after much con-
sultation; and it seemed as though the wooden bonds,
which spanned the river at these two points, instead of
uniting, tended rather to separate the sections. . . .
"You see how the thing is, who's to pay the fiddler!
If the five gentlemen of the West Side say--we won't pay
for your bridges--what did you build them for! what shall
the five gentlemen of the East side do! come, that's the
question! Put their hands in their pockets and toss out
the money! Perhaps so, but the people have something to
say about that! Its a knotty question gentlemen."
The ten gentlemen alluded to were the trustees of
the two wards who met in common council but did very little in common. Each five being as distinct, so far as

co-operation was concerned, as the digitals on either
arm of the physical body. There were two separate corporations to all intents (each tolerating the other,)
which formed the town government. They of the East side
claimed the right to do as they pleased in regard to
their locality, and the West side looked with jealous
eye on any interference with their affairs. Common
good, if not common sense, was overlooked--disregarded
entirely for "home interests."

As the mayor said--who was to pay for the bridges,
that was the question--ultimately to be resolved, so far
as the structures themselves were concerned, into the
more epigrammatic question of "to be or not to be." The
East side had hitherto contributed mainly to the support
of all the bridges, but the precedent never anticipated
the multiplication of bridges indefinitely, and since
the erection of the Wells Street bridge, at the foot of
Oneida Street, there were those taxpayers who stoutly
asserted that ere long the whole stream would be shut
out from the light of day by over-arching Rialto's whose
costly device and absurd luxuriance would involve the East
siders in bankruptcy and ruin--<u>unless the West siders
paid their share</u>. The worthy folk of Kilbourntown said
they had not the "remotest idea of paying for what they
didn't want, but what, in their opinion, was a nuisance."
Thus matters ran along until the spring of 1845, when the
badinage and sarcasm which had been shot across the un-
conscious waters were turned into threats of deeper
meaning. . . .

On the third of May, Capt. Corbitt brought his
schooner in contact with the Spring Street bridge and
partially demolished it, tearing away the draw entirely.
This took place on Saturday afternoon, and as soon as it
became known a sensation was produced on the West side.
The East siders said it was accidental and resulted from
the negligence of the bridge tender in not hanging lights
out--but it was boldly asserted by the opposite neighbors
that a "pony purse" had been made up to induce Capt. Corbitt to commit the act. Though he was arrested, and after
an examination before Justice Walworth, was bound over to
answer before the District Court, nothing ever was done.
The suit was hushed up or dropped, thus establishing in
the minds of many the truth of this assertion. The people of the West ward were highly incensed at the outrage,
and Mr. Kilbourn, when the broken bridge was shown to him,
and the excited bystanders asked him what was best to do
now, replied, "lie down and let the East siders walk over
you." This was understood to be both an injunction to do
no such thing and an implication that it had already been
done. On the night of May seventh, the Board of Trustees
being convened, Mr. Moses Kneeland, from the West Ward,
introduced the following preamble and resolutions:
<u>Whereas</u>, The Chestnut Street bridge was originally

built by the county and suffered to go out of repair and
out of use; and <u>whereas</u>, the said bridge, as regards the
business and convenience of the people of the West Ward,
is deemed by them and the corporate authority of the said
ward to be an insupportable nuisance; and <u>whereas</u>, in
their opinion, there is no lawful power possessed by any
person or corporation to maintain such bridge; therefore
    "<u>Resolved</u>, that the Committee on Streets and Bridges
in the West Ward, be and they are hereby authorized and
required to remove out of the river, so much of the old
county bridge and all appendages thereto as occupy or in
any manner obstruct the free navigation of the Milwaukee
river, west of the middle of said river, and for that
purpose to employ the necessary laborers, either by the
day or by the job, as they may deem expedient. . . ."
    The introduction of these resolutions, retaliatory
as they were, could not fail to produce some sensation.
A debate immediately arose. Mr. Prentiss, of the East
Ward, took exception to their passage on the ground that
one ward had not the power, under the act of incorporation, to declare what was a nuisance, without the assent
of the whole board.
    Mr. Walker, of the South Ward, moved that the pre-
amble and resolutions be laid on the table, but the president decided the motion to be out of order, . . .
    The decision of the chair was finally overruled,
and Mr. Kneeland withdrawing his resolutions--Mr. Kilbourn presented the following:
    "<u>Resolved</u>, That the Committee on Streets and Bridges,
in the West Ward, be and they are hereby authorized and
required to remove out of Chestnut Street so much of the
the old county bridge and all appendages thereto, as occupy any part of said street, and for that purpose to employ the necessary laborers, either by the day or by the
job. as they may deem expedient."
    This resolution was adopted; the West Ward alone
voting. Mr. Gruenbagan immediately tendered his resig-
nation as a member of the Committee on Streets and Bridges, for the West Ward; and Mr. Kilbourn was appointed to
fill the vacancy.
    The news of the action of the Trustees was not cir-
culated on the east side--owing to the late hour at which
the Board adjourned. The primitive habits of the people
sending them to bed shortly after the sun disappeared behind the Menomonee Bluffs. The two or three who lingered
at Sherwood's bristled up properly at the news, but that
the "country people" would dare to carry out their resolutions was not believed; . . .
    Early the next morning, however, rumor arose with
the inhabitants. Ere the shutters had all been taken
down or the matutinal bell had evoked the hungry boarders,
it was reported that the west siders were digging away the
Chestnut Street bridge. Very little time was allowed to

elapse before the citizens were running about in a high
state of excitement; or, as the Major expressed it: "Like
hens with their heads off." Have you heard it? Is it
so? Have they dared? became the interrogations at every
corner. A crowd gradually collected about the corners of
East Water and Wisconsin Streets, on the east side; and
an impromptu meeting appointed a committee to repair immediately to the scene of operations, and learn the truth
of the rumors.

Meanwhile, the excitement grew. The sexton of the
First Presbyterian Church having accumulated a great a-
mount of contradictory intelligence, from the various
corners, came privately to the conclusion that some un-
fathomable horror had burst somewhere; and seizing his
only weapon--the bell rope--he rung out a wild and weird
alarum, which was caught up by the bell on the Milwaukee
House, and re-echoed in a series of metallic yelps, that
indicated to the peaceful inhabitants that a crisis had
taken place in something, somewhere, and they were all
expected to turn out and hunt it up for themselves.

The hubbub seemed to augment by its own exertions,
and if the "Promised Land" had been located across the
river and there had been one plank to reach it, the attempt to nefariously destroy that link could not have created more of a ferment, in less time than did the equally
unwarrantable attempt of the West siders to cut off communication by grading away the terminus of Chestnut
Street.

The committee or delegation that had been sent to
Chestnut Street bridge, found the rumors to be correct.
Sure enough a score of men, with teams, were digging away
manfully at the street on the west side, and fast rendering all connection, between the apron of the bridge and
the bank, a matter of history and memory only. Mr. Harrison Ludington, who was one of the delegation, remon-
strated with the laborers. He informed them that the
people of the east side were in a state of great excitement, as they thought the act unwarranted and illegal.
"So great is the feeling of opposition," he added, "that
I should advise you to look out for your teams, as some
of the mob may shoot them."

The committee hurried back to report, but the grading went on, and the platform connecting with the bridge
fell in. Immediately after the departure of the committee, certain of those then and there employed on the west
side did cause to be circulated a shameful report that
the east siders had threatened to shoot their teams, and
were coming over in a body to perform that gratuitous in-
iquity. A report that did not tend to allay matters, but
had rather a contrary effect, for a crowd gathered about
the men at the bridge, determined to protect their hearth
stones and liberty with their latest breath, aided and
abetted by bludgeons, muskets and horse pistols--all of

which meant that they intended to back up the west siders
in their attempt to render the bridge impassible.

The popular commotion was raging when the deputation
returned; a dangerous sea of humanity, agitated by diverse
currents, and lashed into general fury by winds of passion. . . .

When the gentlemen, who had returned from the bridge,
made an official report, and with unsparing, and exag-
gerated terms, told how the west siders were ruthlessly
destroying the property of the town and throwing disgrace
upon the community, by their reckless and defiant mea-
sures--the waves of this sea leapt up. . . He heard one
man propose, in a stentorian voice, to ride Kneeland on
a rail and a score of undiscoverable throats assented to
the proposition. . . a crowd dragging a small field-piece
down Wisconsin Street, followed by a greater crowd of men,
gesticulating violently. . . the men in charge of the
gun, to aim it at Byron Kilbourn's house, . . . the mob
shouted like wild beasts, and seemed to sway and toss
about in a mad delirium of purpose, to do something out-
rageous and irremediable. . . . Byron Kilbourn was the
obnoxious person to whom the unthinking populace attribu-
ted all their mischief. . . . the responsibility of indi-
viduals was lost in the general exasperation--that the
crowd would commit every unlawful act, perhaps even murder, as a mob--while the members of it as men, would
shrink from the commission of a petty offence at another
time. . . passion had overwhelmed judgment, and a few
fiery words, the appearance of a leader, would precipi-
tate matters, and launch the community into a chasm of
difficulties and disgrace, that years would not efface.
. . .

After several months of war, a feeling of compromise
began to be evinced, and on the night of December 31st,
1845, the belligerents met by their representatives in the
corporation meeting, and a general desire to settle all
the difficulties amicably was apparent. Mr. Prentiss
offered the following resolutions:

Resolved, That a committee of two members of this
board, from the East, and two from the West Ward, be
now appointed, whose duty it shall be, to issue proposals
for the construction of new and permanent bridges across
the Milwaukee river. . .

Resolved, That the expense of constructing, sustain-
ing and attending said bridges, shall be apportioned between said wards, . . .

MAYOR JUNEAU. HIS INAUGURAL AND VALEDICTORY
ADDRESSES -- 1846-1847

In January, 1846 Milwaukee became
a city; Solomon Juneau was inevitably accorded the honor of being
Milwaukee's first mayor. On April
10, 1846 he took his oath, swore
in the aldermen and delivered a
speech written for him by Horatio
Wells. On April 14, 1867, having
passed an uneventful year dealing
with Indian affairs and largely
ignoring the city, Juneau delivered a valedictory address. The
impression left by the speeches
is that of a humble man totally
out of his element.

Source: Wheeler, Chronicles of Milwaukee, 182-187.

GENTLEMEN:--It is made my duty by the charter under
which we have our existence as a municipal corporation,
to recommend to you, in writing, such measures as I may
deem expedient and calculated to advance the interest
of our city.

In performing this duty, I feel conscious that my
burden is light, knowing as I do, that those with whom I
am to co-operate are well versed in all matters pertain-
ing to our welfare. However, as it will be expected on
this occasion that I should make some general remarks
relative to the course to be pursued by us, I shall pro-
ceed in as brief a manner as possible to lay before you
a few general matters that I think should receive an early attention at your hands.

The confusion incident to a change of government,
has rendered it impossible for me to lay before you a
correct statement of our financial condition, but pru-
dence would seem to dictate to us the propriety of ascer-
taining at as early a day as possible the precise state
of the financial affairs of the city, and all proper
efforts in future should be directed to keeping our expenditures within our means, and if it is ascertained
that we are in debt at present, no time should be lost in
taking such measures as will be best calculated to insure
at no distant period a final liquidation of all just
claims against us.

Our commercial interests should receive a proper
share of your attention, and every facility should be af-
forded those engaged in commercial business, to transact
the same in a prompt and efficient manner, and nothing
should be wanting on the part of the city, to render the

whole of the commercial part of it easy of access to the
vessels navigating our lakes.

Proper measures should be taken to render ease of
access of our city to every part of the country around
us, and a due sense of self-respect would seem to suggest to us the propriety of keeping our streets and sidewalks as clear from impediments as the business of the
city will permit.

Such measures as in your wisdom you may think should
be taken to preserve the health of the city; and nothing
should be left undone that would be a tendency to relieve
the distressed and destitute who are incapable of provid-
ing the means of comfort and support for themselves.

The Fire Department should receive your fostering
care, and everything should be done that is calculated to
render those volunteers, serving the city in the capacity
of firemen, secure from injuries by the explosion of pow-
der or other explosive matter.

The subject of gaming should receive your attention,
and nothing in your power should be wanting to secure the
youth of the city from the wiles and devices of the gamb-
ler. Nor should he who is so far regardless of the morals
of a community, as to prostitute the energies of his
mind and body to gaining a livelihood by openly following
the illicit business of gaming, be permitted to range our
streets, unwhipt of justice.

This much I have thought proper to suggest as being
of a public and general nature, trusting fully to your
wisdom and experience in rightly directing all things
relating to our welfare, and in framing such ordinances
as will be best calculated to advance the interest of the
city, fully assuring you, that you will have my cordial
co-operation in every thing tending to promote our common good; and that all in my power will be done to have
the laws of the territory, and ordinances of the city,
properly observed and faithfully and impartially executed.

In performing the duties of presiding officer of
your body, I shall have to ask your indulgence and assistance, knowing that my want of experience in presiding o-
ver deliberative bodies will be sensibly felt by me, and
without your indulgence and friendly counsel I can scarce-
ly hope to execute that part of my official duty in a manner satisfactory to myself or the public. . . .

* * * *

GENTLEMEN:--Before I vacate this chair, I wish to
make a few remarks to your honorable body. When I first
set foot on this soil, some thirty years ago, I little
thought that during my age and generation I should behold
such a sight as now presents itself. Then the red man was
supreme monarch of the place on which our delightful city
now stands, the plains and the rivers of Wisconsin be-
longed to him and were subject to his wild control, but
now the scene has changed; the war whoop of the Indian

has given way to the mild counsels of civilized and intelligent men; the wigwam is supplanted by massive and
ornamental structures; the place of the bark canoe, which
was then the only craft that floated upon the waters of
the noble river that meanders through the heart of your
city, has been filled by the hundreds of vessels pro-
pelled by wind and steam, that now annually visit our
shore and enter our harbor laden with the commerce of
the East and bear off the surplus product of Wisconsin.

Here we behold a city of twelve thousand inhabitants
with her beautiful streets and walks, her fine gardens,
and splendid buildings and her intelligent and enter-
prising population, where eleven years since the soil
was unbroken.

I have been a resident of your city from its first
commencement to the present day, and trust gentlemen you
will do me the justice to believe that its interest,
growth and prosperity have ever been and still are my
dearest desire; that it may continue to increase in size
and population is my sincerest wish. That we may have
wholesome laws and the same well administered, will be
my earnest prayer when I shall have retired from the
honorable and responsible station to which the partiality
of my fellow citizens has elevated me. . . .

ARCHBISHOP JOHN HENNI DESCRIBES MILWAUKEE
1851

        Accurate descriptions of a boom
        town are difficult to obtain.
        The city portrait drawn by Catho-
        lic Archbishop John Henni in his
        January, 1851 letter to the Leo-
        poldine Foundation of Vienna is
        thus of great interest to the his-
        torian.

Source: "Letters of the Right Reverend John Martin Henni
and the Reverend Anthony Urbanck," Wisconsin Magazine
of History, X (September, 1926), 77-81.

     Milwaukee is situated on the shore of Lake Michigan,
in the valley of Michigan /Milwaukee/ River, the waters
of which are hardly pure and are inhabited by numerous
frogs. The place upon which the city stands is marshy,
and hence cellars cannot be constructed. The streets
are, for the most part, not graded, and show numerous
gaps for houses. The houses are mostly wooden barracks
erected on posts about two feet above the ground, so
that the hogs can comfortably wade around under them.
Of stone houses /brick houses/ there are but few. The
price of the city lots, or building plots, has already
been forced up through speculation from 200 to 1000 dollars each. To build a simple wooden one-story house
costs 700 dollars. One would suppose that in this building of houses many men would find employment, but such
is not the case. From base to ridgepole everything comes
finished from the factory. One gets boards for the floors
already planed, windows with frames and glass, doors with
locks,--in short, everything is prepared by machinery,
and only a few laborers are needed to erect a complete
building out of the several parts. In general, there are
no carpenters in North America, because the joiners can
easily build and join the houses with this ready finished
material. Such wooden houses are often seen "travelling"
through the streets. This means that, if to an American
the place where his house stands seems no longer suffi-
ciently desirable, he has it placed on rollers and pulled
to a better location; he has "moved," as ordinary par-
lance has it. However, during this jaunty trip (which
sometimes lasts eight days) the owner lives in the building, quite comfortable. Rents are rather high. For an
unfinished room one pays ordinarily a dollar and a half.
Furniture is very expensive; a table costs from four to
six dollars, a bedstead, from six to eight dollars, and a
chair, from one half to two dollars. The price of food

is cheap--twelve to fifteen cents a meal. . . .

There are many Germans here, so that one may speak
German in nearly every store or inn.

Life in this city is very provincial, since everybody concerns himself about the financial condition, family relations, and religious profession of every other
inhabitant, and tries to know all of them. For this purpose questions which seem proper are directed to new ar-
rivals. There are about twenty churches and houses of
prayer here, belonging to different denominations, such
as the Methodists, Episcopalians, Lutherans, Evangeli-
cals, Bible Christians, etc., etc.

The factories here are interesting on account of
their simple and sensible machines. In these, as in the
entire field of American activity, it must be admitted
that there prevails a certain perfunctory way of doing
things, which admits of no comparison with German ex-
actness and solidity. But there is here a progressive,
inventive spirit; and what is new with us in Germany has
here been discarded long since, or improved. While with
us a machine is built to last twenty years, it is here
unserviceable in a few years; and the American builds another, applying on it all the knowledge gained by using
the old one.

Taste for art is still in its infancy. Artists do
not stay here, and they would be disappointed if they
did. Of architecture there is also not a trace; building
is done hurriedly, not beautifully nor solidly. In
three weeks an American completes a two-story frame house,
that is, a cabin of boards and planks; and in six weeks
an even larger brick house. Since, as mentioned before,
the ground is quite marshy, water is reached by digging
two or three feet down; hence cellars are found only on
elevations. Now, upon this marshy ground planks are laid,
and the masonry is erected on the planks. As a result,
seams and cracks--running vertically and horizontally--
are often found in these houses when completed only three
weeks. But the American does not mind this--as long as
the building holds together all is well. Of architecture
proper they have no idea, although every house is built
according to a certain style. A frieze, or a few Doric
half-columns nailed on a frame house is considered an
ornament in Grecian, Italian, or East Indian style. To
class yourself as an architect here, you have to be, at
the same time, a building contractor; this means that
you must have sufficient money to take over the contract
for the erection of the building. Generally speaking,
only two classes of builders do good business here: the
man who is supplied with capital for his enterprises; and
the craftsman who, having some property, establishes himself independently.

The peasant, or farmer, here feel happy if only he
has sufficient to live upon, possesses a few head of cat-

tle and a frame cabin. Usually he cannot exchange his
products for cash, but finds a customer who will make
an exchange in trade--a quite customary practice here.
By making cash payments a buyer always obtains a dis-
count equivalent to one-third the value of the goods
purchased. While on this subject I will insert a few
words on taxes.

The people here praise the low and insignificant
taxes as a particular reason why business can grow rapidly
and the farmers grow wealthy. Many entertain a concep-
tion of freedom from taxes, which in reality does not
exist. In our American state of Wisconsin the following
conditions prevail: The citizens are taxed according to
property and income. An alderman or councilman comes
during the month of July each year, to the individual
citizens, and has them report on good faith their annual
receipts; he then appraises the real estate and buildings.
According to this finding, every business man or property
owner is taxed at the rate of 4 or 5 per cent within the
city limits, and the farmers 1 to 2 per cent. . . .

With respect to the ecclesiastical situation and the
conditions of pastoral care in the city of Milwaukee there
is a Catholic population of 20,000 souls or more, and
already four Catholic churches, with a fifth soon to
follow. It is my endeavor to make Milwaukee a Catholic
city. Five years ago I undertook, under most adverse
circumstances, to build the beautiful St. Mary's Church
in the First Ward; and, with God's protection and bles-
sing, we completed it. German immigrants streamed into
Milwaukee, so that at the end of one year this church could
not, even then, accomodate more than half the number of
the faithful hastening thither. It therefore became
necessary to build a second House of God (a frame building), St. Gall's. I chose for this the Fifth Ward, for
the reason that the settlements here were, as yet, quite
rare, and the grounds for the erection of a church, as
well as for purchase by every immigrant, were still toler-
ably cheap. The result was that here also a considerable
number of the faithful very soon settled, and affiliated
themselves with the new parish. Then the need for a new
church--that of the Blessed Trinity--became apparent. The
building was commenced and completed, the length being
220 feet and the breadth 80 feet. It is built of bricks.
. . .

But, beside the pressing debt of 4000 dollars, the
interior is furnished only with an altar, and is without
organ, steeple, and even a bell to announce the call of
redemption to those dwelling around. The visitor enter-
ing the church is greeted by naked whitewashed walls.
Hence, all anxiously await help from abroad.

ANTHONY TROLLOPE VISITS "A VERY PLEASANT TOWN"
1862

> The English novelist Anthony Trol-
> lope traveled across America during
> the first months of our Civil War.
> He was impressed, almost in spite
> of himself, with the vitality and
> beauty of Milwaukee -- especially
> when he compared it to other Amer-
> ican cities.

Source: Anthony Trollope, <u>North America</u>, Philadelphia:
J. B. Lippincott, 1862, 130-136.

From Detroit we continued our course westward across
the State of Michigan, through a country that was absolutely wild till the railway pierced it. Very much of it
is still absolutely wild. For miles upon miles the road
passes the untouched forest, showing that even in Michigan the great work of civilization has hardly more than
been commenced. As one thinks of the all but countless
population which is, before long, to be fed from these
regions--of the cities which will grow here, and of the
amount of government which in due time will be required--
one can hardly fail to feel that the division of the United States into separate nationalities is merely a part
of the ordained work of creation as arranged for the well-
being of mankind. . . .
Our route lay right across the State to a place
called Grand Haven, on Lake Michigan, from whence we were
to take boat for Milwaukee, a town in Wisconsin, on the
opposite or western shore of the lake. Michigan is sometimes called the Peninsular State, from the fact that the
main part of its territory is surrounded by Lakes Michigan and Huron, by the little Lake St. Clair and by Lake
Erie. It juts out to the northward from the main land of
Indiana and Ohio, and is circumnavigable on the east,
north and west. These particulars, however, refer to a
part of the State only; for a portion of it lies on the
other side of Lake Michigan, between that and Lake Su-
perior. I doubt whether any large inland territory in
the world is blessed with such facilities of water carriage. . . .
Milwaukee is a pleasant town, a very pleasant town,
containing 45,000 inhabitants. How many of my readers
can boast that they know anything of Milwaukee, or even
have heard of it? To me its name was unknown until I saw
it on huge railway placards stuck up in the smoking-rooms
and lounging halls of all American hotels. It is the big
town of Wisconsin, whereas Madison is the capital. It

stands immediately on the western shore of Lake Michigan, and is very pleasant. Why it should be so, and why Detroit should be the contrary, I can hardly tell; only I think that the same verdict would be given by any English tourist. It must always be borne in mind that 10,000 or 40,000 inhabitants in an American town, and especially in any new Western town, is a number which means much more than would be implied by any similar number as to an old town in Europe. Such a population in America consumes double the amount of beef which it would in England, wears double the amount of clothes, and demands double as much of the comforts of life. If a census could be taken of the watches, it would be found, I take it, that the American population possessed among them nearly double as many as would the English; and I fear also that it would be found that many more of the Americans were readers and writers by habit. In any large town in England it is probable that a higher excellence of education would be found than in Milwaukee, and also a style of life into which more of refinement and more of luxury had found its way. But the general level of these things, of material and intellectual well-being--of beef that is, and book learning--is no doubt infinitely higher in a new American than in an old European town. . . .

The founders of cities have had the experience of the world before them. They have known of sanitary laws as they began. That sewerage, and water, and gas, and good air would be needed for a thriving community has been to them as much a matter of fact as are the well-understood combinations between timber and nails, and bricks and mortar. They have known that water carriage is almost a necessity for commercial success, and have chosen their sites accordingly. Broad streets cost as little, while land by the foot is not yet of value to be regarded as those which are narrow; and therefore the sites of towns have been prepared with noble avenues and imposing streets. A city at its commencement is laid out with an intention that it shall be populous. The houses are not all built at once, but there are the places allocated for them. The streets are not made, but there are the spaces. Many an abortive attempt at municipal greatness has been so made and then all but abandoned. There are wretched villages, with huge, straggling parallel ways, which will never grow into towns. They are the failures--failures in which the pioneers of civilization, frontier men as they call themselves, have lost their tens of thousands of dollars. But when the success comes, when the happy hit has been made, and the ways of commerce have been truly forseen with a cunning eye, then a great and prosperous city springs up, ready made as it were, from the earth. Such a town is Milwaukee, now containing 45,000 inhabitants, but with room apparently for double that number; with room for four times that number, were men packed as closely there as they are with us.

In the principal business streets of all these towns
one sees vast buildings. They are usually called blocks,
and are often so denominated in large letters on their
front, as Portland Block, Devereux Block, Buel's Block.
Such a block may face two, three, or even four streets,
and, as I presume, has generally been a matter of one
special speculation. It may be divided into separate
houses, or kept for a single purpose, such as that of a
hotel, or grouped into shops below, and into various sets
of chambers above. I have had occasion in various towns
to mount the stairs within these blocks, and have generally found some portion of them vacant--have sometimes
found the greater portion of them vacant. Men build on
an enormous scale, three times, ten times as much as is
wanted. The only measure of size is an increase on what
men have built before. Monroe P. Jones, the speculator,
is very probably ruined, and then begins the world again,
nothing daunted. But Jones's block remains, and gives
to the city in its aggregate a certain amount of wealth.
. . .

It may be imagined how large in proportion to its
inhabitants will be a town which spreads itself in this
way. There are great houses left untenanted, and great
gaps left unfilled. But if the place be successful, if
it promise success, it will be seen at once that there is
life all through it. Omnibuses, or street cars working
on rails, run hither and thither. The shops that have
been opened are well filled. The great hotels are
thronged. The quays are crowded with vessels, and a general feeling of progress pervades the place. It is easy
to perceive whether or no an American town is going ahead.
The days of my visit to Milwaukee were days of civil war
and national trouble, but in spite of civil war and national trouble Milwaukee looked healthy.

WILLARD GLAZIER ASSESSES THE "CREAM CITY
OF THE LAKES" -- 1883

In the boom years after the War,
Milwaukee turned its economy from
commerce toward manufacturing. In
his analysis of the 1880 census,
Willard Glazier not only assessed
the city's business but also re-
marked on its ethnic characteris-
tics. He described a bustling metropolis which successfully acculturated the thousands of immigrants
who thronged to its shore.

Source: <u>Peculiarities of American Cities</u>, Philadelphia:
Hubbard Brothers, 1883, 223-227.

. . . . /Milwaukee/ has other iron works, and manufactures machinery, agricultural implements, car wheels
and steam boilers, large quantities of tobacco and ci-
gars; furnishes the Northwest with furniture, and has extensive pork packing establishments, while the products
of her flouring mills and lager beer breweries find markets in every quarter of the United States, and have a
reputation all their own. The rolling mill of the North
Chicago Rolling Mill Company is one of the most extensive
in the West.
As a grain depot, Milwaukee takes high rank. There
are six immense elevators within the limits of the city,
with a united capacity of 3,450,000 bushels; the largest
one, the grain elevator of the Milwaukee and St. Paul
Railroad, being one of the largest on the continent, and
having a storage capacity of 1,500,000 bushels. The
flour mills of E. Sanderson & Company have a daily capacity of one thousand barrels of flour.
The harbor of Milwaukee is the best on the south or
west shore of Lake Michigan. It is formed by the mouth
of the Milwaukee River, and the largest lake boat can
ascend it for two miles, to the heart of the city, at
which point the Menomonee River unites with the Milwaukee. The course of the Milwaukee River is nearly due
south, while that of the Menomonee is nearly due west;
and by these two rivers and their united stream after
their junction, the city is divided into three very nearly equal districts, which are severally known as the
East, being that portion of the city between the Milwaukee River and Lake Michigan; the West, that portion included between the two rivers; and the South, or the
territory south of them both. The city embraces an area
of seventeen square miles, and is laid out with the re-

gularity characteristic of western cities. The business
quarter lies in a sort of hollow in the neighborhood of
the two rivers, whose shores are lined with wharves. The
East and West portions of the city are chiefly occupied
by residences, the former being upon a high bluff, over-
looking the lake, and the latter upon a still higher
bluff west of the river.
     Milwaukee is known as the "Cream City of the Lakes,"
this name being derived from the cream-colored brick of
which many of the buildings are constructed. It gives
to the streets a peculiarly light and cheerful aspect.
The whole architectural appearance of the city is one of
primness rather than of grandeur, which might not inap-
propriately suggest for it the name of the "Quaker City
of the West." The residence streets are shaded by avenues of trees, which add to the cheerful beauty of the
town. The principal hotels and retail stores are found
upon East Water street, Wisconsin street and Second avenue, which are all three wide and handsome thoroughfares.
The United States Custom House stands on the corner of
Wisconsin and Milwaukee streets, and is the finest public
building in the city. It is of Athens stone, and contains
the Post Office and United States Courts. The County
Court House is also a striking edifice. The Opera House,
used for theatrical purposes, is worthy of mention; while
the Academy of Music, which was erected in 1864, by the
German Musical Society, at a cost of $65,000, has an ele-
gant auditorium, seating two thousand three hundred persons. The Roman Catholic Cathedral of St. John, and the
new Baptist Church, are fine church edifices, but the finest which the city contains is the Immanuel Presbyterian
Church. A Free Public Library possesses a collection of
fourteen thousand volumes, and a well-supplied reading
room. Several banking houses have imposing buildings.
The most prominent among the educational institutions of
the city is the Milwaukee Female College, which was finished in 1873. There are three Orphan Asylums, a Home
for the Friendless, and two Hospitals. One of the
chief points of interest to the visitor is the Northwestern National Asylum for disabled soldiers, which furnishes excellent accomodation for from seven hundred to
eight hundred inmates. It is an immense brick edifice,
located three miles from the city, in the midst of grounds
four hundred and twenty-five acres in extent, more than
half of which is under cultivation, and the remainder
laid out as a park. The institution has a reading room,
and a library of two thousand five hundred volumes, for
the use and benefit of its patriot guests.
     No one who visits Milwaukee can fail to be struck
with the semi-foreign appearance of the city. Breweries
are multiplied throughout its streets, lager beer saloons
abound, beer gardens, with their flowers and music and
cleanly arbor-shaded tables, attract the tired and thirsty

in various quarters. German music halls, gasthausen,
and restaurants are found everywhere, and German signs
are manifest over many doors. One hears German spoken
upon the streets quite as often as English, and Teuton
influence upon the political and social life of the city
is everywhere seen and felt. Germans constitute nearly
one-half the entire population of Milwaukee, and have impressed their character upon the people and the city itself in other ways than socially. Steady-going plodders,
with their love for music and flowers, they have yet no
keen taste for display, and every time choose the substantial rather than the ornamental. Milwaukee is a sort of
rendezvous for the Scandinavian emigrants, who are pour-
ing in like a mighty tide to fill up the States of Wisconsin and Minnestoa. Danes and Swedes, and especially
Norwegians, stop here, and it may be, linger for a longer
or shorter period, before they strike out into the, to
them, unknown country which is to be their future home.
Domestic service is largely supplied by the Norwegians,
who prove themselves honest, industrious and capable.

This mighty influx of the Germanic and Scandinavian
races into our Northwest is certain to produce a permanent impression upon the social condition of those States,
Yet our system of government is adapted to the successful
management of such immigration. It cannot, perhaps, do
so much with the immigrants themselves. Many of them intelligent, but more of them ignorant and stupid, they remain foreign in their habits and ideas to the end of their
lives. But it makes citizens of their sons, trains them
up with an understanding of democratic institutions, gives
them an education, for the most part, forces them to acquire our language, and instead of making them a separate
class, recognizes them as an undivided part of the whole
population. In brief, it Americanizes them, and though
habits and traits of character and race still cling to
them in some degree, their original nationality is soon
lost. . . .

THE "CREAM CITY" OF 1891
1891

Another laudatory analysis, but
one with overtones of bigotry,
boosterism and self-satisfaction,
was offered by Charles King. In
the eyes of its citizens, Milwaukee was destined to continue always prosperous, safe and content.

Source: Charles King, "The Cream City," Cosmopolitan, X
(March, 1891), 554-557.

Start at the southern line, and leaving behind a
big Polack settlement just outside the limits, where no-
body pays city taxes but everybody manages to vote, you
read no names but those that end with a sneeze. Northward as you go, the frontiers of Poland merge in those
of Prussian Pomerania, even as they do along the banks
of the Vistula. Fritz appears in place of Ignatz. The
signs of the times and of the south side point to foreign
supremacy. But just wait until you have crossed the Menomonee, traversed the long canon of West Water street,
whereon are the great wholesale houses and really quite
a sprinkling of American names, and emerge once more into
sunshine and Deutschland! Here, advancing no matter how
many parasangs northward, the explorer may revel in the
belief that he is indeed in Germany. Not an English or
American name is on the signs. Indeed, there are shops
in whose windows not long ago appeared the encouraging
legend, "English spoken here," and there are other shops
where, even today, such a sign would be misleading. You
can enter those where not one word of English, by the inmates at least, is spoken. The southwestern section of
our city is all Poland; the northwestern all Germany.
The few Irish we have congregate mostly in the old third
ward. The German and Polish population outnumbers the
native probably three to one, and in nine cases out of
ten this might be a cause for alarm, but--not in Milwaukee.
Polack, Hungarian, Prussian, Bavarian, Wurtemburger,
it makes no difference. There is not of its size in all
America a city that contains a population more self-re-
specting, more law-abiding, more cheerful and content
than Milwaukee, and you have only to ride or drive through
these great sections to see the reason--there isn't a
real tenement house in the town. Almost every family has
its own little home. In proportion to population Milwaukee stands foremost in our nation in the number of dwel-
lings owned by the occupants, and no matter how humble it

may be, it is the home that makes the citizen who has the
public interests at heart. There are no slums in Milwaukee; no thronging rookeries of misery and vice. The
poor have we always with us, as is the case with every
community, but they herd not like cattle. Even they have
their little roof and fireside. We have, of course, in
some sections, the irrepresible street boy and an occa-
sional corner loafer, but their wildest exploits are mo-
dels of good manners as compared with the daily performances of the "toughs" of Chicago or the hoodlums of San
Francisco. We had, as was to be expected in so large a
foreign element, a gang of anarchists, who were allowed
to scream themselves hoarse at their lurid meetings, to
parade the streets with red flags and ragged integuments,
shouting defiance to law and death to capitalists; but
the very first time they overstepped the mark and sought
to level or destroy, our guardsmen gave them one volley
and they haven't been heard of since. In time of insur-
rection blank cartridges are forbidden in the Badger
state and so are volleys in the air.

    Politically we are the most impartial community you
ever heard of. Our one representative in Congress assembled is chosen, apparently, with the view of giving all
parties a show. Four years ago we sent the Labor candidate, two years ago the Republican, this year we chose
the Democrat; and no man in the community can prophesy
the future other than this, that Milwaukee will never
send a prohibitionist. We have more saloons than any
city of our size in the world--and less drunkenness.
Why? Because nine-tenths of our people drink good, wholesome, homemade beer, and let whiskey severly alone. We
have a smaller death rate, smaller taxes, smaller percen-
tage of murders, assaults, robberies, burglaries, larcen-
ies and drunks, and a smaller police force; we have smaller and fewer fires, and a smaller fire department than
any city of our size in the land, and we can prove it by
the records. We have 40,000 homes for our 220,000 people,
and there is abundant room for more. We did have trouble
with our big central sewer in hot weather, as has been
mentioned. Its "offence was rank and smelt to heaven."
We sent for the first sanitary engineers of the country,
and they could devise no scheme but the fearfully costly
one of intercepting sewers. Our own engineer declared
that he could bore a hole through the bluffs, pump the
pure lake water into the murky Mahn-a-wauk, wash it out
and give it a permanent current. The experts said it
couldn't be done, but it was; and it hasn't given us a
smell to speak of since. Of course the expedient is but
temporary. The bottom of our river is foul with the de-
posit of a thousand sewers, and sooner or later, as city
and suburbs grow, the intercepting system will probably
prevail.

    Out in the broad Menomonee valley are placed the

slaughter houses, the mammoth beef and prok packeries, the tanneries, rendering vats, soap and candle shops and other malodorous trades; but no one is inconvenienced thereby except those south and west siders who dwell within sniffing range of the valley, and consequently have the profound commiseration and best advice of those of us who do not. Over on the east side, extending to Whitefish bay, are whole tracts of homestead lands, platted and graded, with the lake breezes sweeping over them, the lake banks on the east, the wooded shores of the river on the west. It is one of the loveliest tracts of all the neighborhood, and thither our beautiful city is bound to grow.

Nor is Milwaukee, despite its shops and foundries, a smoky city. Nearly 2000 manufacturing establishments have we. Nearly 50,000 hands are employed. Nearly 100 articles of commercial value are turned out by her various firms, and the greatest of these is Beer. Ten million dollars' worth of beef, pork, etc., was packed in the big houses two years ago, but more than that amount of the amber fluid sacred to Gambrinus was bottled or barrelled. Milwaukee bricks, whose pale straw color gave to her the sobriquet of the Cream City, are known throughout the country. Milwaukee beer is known the world over. Milwaukee's breweries have no superiors in the States, and one of them, the Pabst, is the biggest lager-beer plant on the globe. Over 600,000 barrels were its last year's product, and if its floor space could be spread out it would cover nearly thirty acres. There is simply no use in trying to describe it in an article of this size. Its vaults are tunnelled out from under the heights of the west side. Its buildings seem to leap from block to block, for, high in air, over the busiest streets, they are banded together by bridges of iron. The establishment is a municipality in itself.

Down on the south side, on the once narrow strip called "Walker's Point," are the Reliance Works, the Bay State works and the various foundries, all of the E. P. Allis company, and there every manner of engine is made. Minneapolis grinds the wheat of the wide Northwest, but Milwaukee makes her mills. Here are built the great Corliss engines. Here New York city, Albany, Omaha, Boston, Providence, even Chicago come for their triple-expansion engines. All was swamp where now the hum of wheels and whir of belt, the clang of ponderous machinery, the glare of huge furnaces, tell of the presence of the busiest industry. . . .

LINCOLN STEFFENS ON MILWAUKEE
1904

> Milwaukee offered not only commer-
> cial and industrial advantages,
> but also the controversial vices
> available along River Street. Un-
> der David Rose, five times elected
> mayor, the city offered business-
> men and conventioneers the hospi-
> tality of an American Sodom for
> which no apology was necessary.
> Rose's "wide open" town did not
> go unnoticed. When Lincoln Stef-
> fens visited Milwaukee, he con-
> demned it roundly; it was "St.
> Louis all over again." Steffens
> analyzed the working alliance be-
> tween city government and big
> business.

Source: "Enemies of the Republic," McClure's Magazine,
XXII (October, 1904), 577-578.

District Attorney Bennett has had grand juries at
work in Milwaukee since 1901, and he has some 42 persons
indicted--12 aldermen, 10 supervisors, 9 other officials,
1 state senator, and 10 citizens; four convictions and
three pleas of guilty. The grafting so far exposed is
petty, but the evidence in hand indicates a highly per-
fected noodle system. The Republicans had the county,
the Democrats the city, and both the council and the
board of supervisors had combines which grafted on contracts, public institutions, franchises, and other business privileges. The corrupt connection of business and
politics was shown; the informants were merchants and con-
tractors, mostly small men, who confessed to bribery.
The biggest caught so far is Colonel Pabst, the brewer,
who paid a check of $1,500 for leave to break a building
law. But all signs point higher than beer, to more "le-
gitimate" political business. As in Chicago, a bank is
the center of graft, and public utility companies are
back of it. The politicians in the boards of management,
now or formerly, show that. It is a bi-partizan system
all through. Henry C. Payne, while chairman of the Republican State Central Committee, and E. C. Wall (the
man the Wisconsin Democracy offered the National Democratic Convention for President of the United States),
while chairman of the Democratic State Central Committee,
engineered a consolidation of Milwaukee street railway
and electric lighting companies, and, when the job was

done, Payne became manager of the street railway, Wall
of the light company. But this was "business." There
was no scandal about it.

The great scandal of Milwaukee was the extension of
street railway franchises, and the men who put that
through were Charles F. Pfister, the Stalwart Republican
boss, and David S. Rose, the Stalwart Democratic mayor.
Money was paid; the extension was boodled through. The
Milwaukee <u>Sentinel</u> reprinted a paragraph saying Pfister,
among others, did the bribing and thus it happened that
the Stalwarts got that paper. Pfister sued for libel,
but when the editors (now on the Milwaukee <u>Free Press</u>)
made answer that their defense would be proof of the
charge, the millionaire traction man bought the paper and
its evidence too. It is no more than fair to add--as
Milwaukee newspaper men always do (with delight)--that
the paper had very little evidence, not nearly so much
as Pfister seemed to think it had. As for Mayor Rose,
his friends declare that he has told them, personally
and convincingly, that he got not one cent for his service. But that is not the point. Mayor Rose fought to
secure for special interests a concession which sacri-
ficed the common interests of the city. I am aware that
he defends the terms of the grants as fair, and they
would seem so in the East, but the West is intelligent
on special privileges, and Mayor Rose lost to Milwaukee
the chance Chicago seized to settle the public utility
problem. Moreover, Rose knew that his council was corrupt before it was proven so; he told two business men
that they couldn't get a privilege they sought honestly
from him, without bribing aldermen. Yet he ridiculed as
"hot air" an investigation which nevertheless produced
evidence enough to defeat at the polls, in a self-respec-
ting city, the head of an administration so besmirched.
Milwaukee re-elected Rose; good citizens say they gave
the man the benefit of the doubt--the man, not the city.

But this is not the only explanation. The System
was on trial with Mayor Rose in that election, and the
System saved its own. The Republicans, with the Rose
administration exposed, had a chance to win, and they
nominated a good man, Mr. Guy D. Goff. Pfister, the
Stalwart Republican boss, seemed to support Goff; certainly the young candidate had no suspicion to the contrary. He has now, however. When the returns came in
showing that he was beaten, Mr. Goff hunted up Mr. Pfister and he found him. Mr. Goff, the Republican candidate for mayor, found Charles F. Pfister, the Stalwart
Republican boss, rejoicing over the drinks with the elected Democratic mayor, David S. Rose.

ZONA GALE DESCRIBES "THE SPIRIT OF THE CITY"
1910

> It was not all graft and gemutlich-
> keit of course. Zona Gale, later a
> Pulitzer Prize winner, also sought
> to understand the new Milwaukee.
> She discovered a reality far great-
> er than graft, the sleaziness of
> machine politics, or even whipped
> cream. It was a modern metropolis
> emerging from pioneer origins.

Source: Zona Gale, "Milwaukee," <u>Good Housekeeping</u>, L
(March, 1910), 317-325.

The curve of the water boundary of the town is ex-
quisitely like a gesture; like the gesture of a lady,
gracious, reticent, somewhat withdrawn even in welcome, a
gesture which is like her signature set upon her meaning.
And sometimes--but this is at night--this harbor line is
a gesture of the spirit of the city, hovering on the bor-
der of the indeterminate waste of the lake, waiting to
be born. For the spirit of Milwaukee, like that of nearly all our American cities, is not yet wholly incarnate.
Partly this line of the shore is defined by railway
tracks, as if Commerce thus made a rude picture to show
how she has knit the city to the distance. Partly it is
bordered by a terraced park and by ordered lawns whose
great houses look sadly down on the ties and rails which
ruin their once yellow beach. And partly the line is
made by the far, south-flung arm of Bay View, indolently
cherishing a sheaf of chimneys which nightly flower in
red glories when the rolling mills set cloud and wave a-
bloom. The tenuous breakwater, its terminal clasped by
the lightship, does not mar the fine, definite beckoning
concavity of the shore. This line of the shore is the
<u>motif</u> of the town, infinitely repeated in drives, in
boulevards, in chains of lights, in ways of trees, in the
splendid avenue which borders the lake. And through this
softening influence dissolves and the westerly streets
stiffen into fingers indicating the compass points and
blocking trig squares, yet the town never altogether loses
its sense of shore, its consciousness of the water. . . .
For the important thing about Milwaukee is not its
magnetic charm, made of home and beauty and much order;
nor is it any phase of the town's material life. But
it is that within a little while great factors have begun to move in relation to one another, and are struggling in new birth. Milwaukee, in a word, almost within the last year has come to civic consciousness, has

begun to find itself, to passion for being and expression
as a component, vital, social part of a recognized whole:
to come alive.

It is a great moment when this experience come to
a soul or to a city. Indefinable and cosmic forces lead
to such a moment, and long, devoted effort on the part of
the pioneer few. In Milwaukee, the efforts which have
resolved themselves into a social consciousness have been
many and many, and one can confidently point to this
source of power and to that. Chief among these, here as
everywhere, has been attention to the cry of the child:
the well-established juvenile court and the work of the
truancy and probation officers; playgrounds in every
large park--even in Kosciuszko Park, in the Polish District, where there was a great municipal fight before the
University Settlement got the playground in and where
there would now be a great people's riot if it were taken
out; natatoriums in every crowded district; the free use
of bathing beaches; four social centers established in the
public schools, with cooking schools in every center, o-
pen evenings to parochial pupils and to factory girls; tu-
berculin-test milk ordinances, among the best and the best
enforced of those of any city; the trade schools; weekly
summer concerts in all the parks, so that there are no
more beer gardens, for the parks have the people and the
music; the social settlements; the Visiting Nurses' Association; the work of the city health department and others
in city housing and tuberculosis prevention; the birth of
civics clubs and their federation; the Associated Charities; the brave speech of certain city pulpits; dance
hall regulation; industrial education--all the many-sided
philanthropic life of a city somewhat blindly reaching out
as its people quicken to this and that human fellowship.

And suddenly--like The Ship That Found Herself--all
these strivings have taken to themselves a common life,
the consciousness of the ned of a common civic program.
. . .

"For the common welfare." This modern cry from
hearth and market sounds spiritual life wherever it is
uttered, and wherever it is not yet uttered there is, in
home or heart or town, a spiritual sleeping.

In Milwaukee the cry has been uttered. Its first
note was struck several years ago in some splendid clean-
ing up of municipal graft. It comes now in a more human
message. It will come again and again in the attacks upon abuses which still prevail. For there is still grave
political corruption in Milwaukee; there are those among
its citizens who fought openly against the recent passage
of the Wisconsin nine hour child labor law: there are
housing conditions among some of its factory operatives
lately rebuked by the Wisconsin branch of the American
Federation for Labor Legislation, there are certain of its
great stores which mean disgrace to its underpaid women

employees, so that the patronage of intelligent people is
in a fair way to be withdrawn; there is no little rough-
riding by various public service corporations; and the
abuses of greed are in Milwaukee as they are abroad in
the land. But unutterable things are beginning to utter
themselves; and by the tremendous new tide of national
social undertsanding Milwaukee is being magnificently
swept.

On the extreme upper edge of the high lakeward ter-
races which make Juneau Park there is a statue of Lief
Ericsson. Thrown against the far blue of the sky and
water whence his ship has drawn him, the graceful, spirited figure shades eyes with hand to look over the land
which he has dreamed true from out the void. More than
anything in Milwaukee, that statue means the town itself--
the vigorous, bold efficient pioneer, robust and daring
of body and mind, and still somewhat astonished at the
rush of its own arrival. But now it is as if the time
had come for this hardy figure to look, not at the so-
vereign marshaling of homes and institutions and industries, but to where, emerging from the future, comes
another pioneer, this time a spirit, the spirit of the
city ready to be born.

HOW REVOLUTIONARY WERE MILWAUKEE'S SOCIALISTS?
1910

> In the elections of April 1910,
> Milwaukee voters rebelled against
> the corruption and scandal that
> had become endemic in their city;
> they put a Socialist administra-
> tion into power. Frederick Howe,
> a city planner and reformer, won-
> dered just how revolutionary the
> change would be.

Source: "Milwaukee, a Socialist City," The Outlook,
95 (June, 1910), 411-421.

Emil Seidel will give Milwaukee clean government.
Of that I am sure. Milwaukee needs it. He will stamp
out graft, waste, and the spoils system. His eight years'
record in the Council and the appointments already made
give assurance of that. He will do many good things that
all agree should be done. He will humanize the city, and
relieve of some of their burdens the lives of those who
toil. But he will not inaugurate the Co-operative Com-
monwealth. He will not usher in the City for the Workers.
At least not during the next two years. . . .

The business men tell me that the officials of Milwaukee are in chains. So are the people for that matter.
Only the Legislature can set them free. And the business
men are satisfied with the present charter. They killed
the Home Rule is dangerous to the interests.

That is one reason why the business men are more or
less indifferent over the election of April 5. Quite a
number of those with whom I talked seemed really pleased.
They spoke of it much as might an indulgent father who had
permitted his son to smoke. It would satisfy his curio-
sity. It would surely make him sick. It might cure him
of the desire for tobacco. So the business men of Milwaukee, whom I expected to find in a state of panic and
protest, seem to view the recent election which swept
the old parties off the stage and carried into office a
straight Socialist administration in the city as well as
in the county. Not only was a Socialist Mayor elected,
but twenty-one Aldermen out of thirty-five, as well as
the City Solicitor, the Comptroller, the Treasurer, two
Civil Judges, and the majority of the County Supervisors.
. . .

There was little split voting. The election was a
clean sweep. And the result seems to have been pretty
generally expected. The people were tired, if not dis-

gusted, with the incompetence, the lack of ideals, and
the allegiance of the two old parties to the public service corporations. The Mayor had been neglecting his
office and the city was drifting.

There had been no graft exposures during the past
two years. The election was not a sudden revulsion a-
gainst disclosures of rottenness, but the people wanted
a new deal. . . .

Did the people of Milwaukee vote for the principles
of Karl Marx, or did they merely elect a body of men
whom they had come to trust, whom they felt to be honest,
industrious, and inspired with different ideals than the
members of the old parties? Opinions differ. Men believe what they want to believe. "Are there twenty-
seven thousand Socialists in Milwaukee?" I asked of one
business man after another. "No," the business men said;
"it is merely a protest of disgust against the old machines, their methods and incompetency. We have had
twelve years of misrule, during ten of which the city
has been in the hands of the Democratic party, under the
control of Mayor David S. Rose. Then there is the general unrest of the country, the protest against the high
cost of living, the trusts, and the monopolies. This is
but another form of the Wisconsin idea which was started
by La Follette, and which has been growing more and more
radical ever since." . . .

But the new administration will do many notable
things. I am convinced that it will make good. Its emphasis will be placed on humanizing life, on the widest
possible consideration for the working classes. The inaugural message of Mayor Seidel emphasized these things.
He said: "The workers of our city are its most valuable
asset. Your attention should be directed to the passage
of such measures as will promote the well-being of this
class of citizens." . . .

There was nothing revolutionary in the message.
Even the platform of the party, which went into much
greater detail than the message of the Mayor, advocated
palliatives rather than cures for the industrial problems
of the day. It was purely local, and had but short reference to the revolutionary programme which occupies so
large a space in the party's National declarations. Here
is what it pledged its candidate to:

1. Complete Home Rule in municipal matters, with the
Initiative, Referendum, and Recall under proper limitations.

2.   The ownership and control of the public service
corporations. In order to make this possible, the modi-
fication of the debt limit of the city so that they may
be acquired.

3.   The establishment of a terminal station with
docks and wharves along the lake, and a belt line surrounding the city in connection with it.

4.   The erection of municipal abattoirs, markets, and a series of cold storage plants by means of which the price of the necessities of life can be controlled by municipal competition.

5.   The maintenance of a public garbage disposal plant.

6.   The taxation of all property-owners, and especially the privileged corporations on the same basis as other property.

7.   The abolition of the contract system and the establishment of a public works department for the doing of city work by direct labor.

8.   An eight-hour day in all city work.

9.   The making of provision for public work for the unemployed. The establishment of a municipal ice plant, and the opening up of coal and wood yards and stone quarries by means of which work can be supplied, and these necessities supplied the people at cost.

10.   The annexation of suburban territory. . . .

DANIEL WEBSTER HOAN DESCRIBES HIS ACCOMPLISHMENTS
1924

In April 1924, Sociliast Daniel
Webster Hoan completed eight
years as mayor. His report to
the common council modestly described the "Golden Age" of progress he had supervised. City
manufacturing alone surpassed
the billion dollar level, while
a new civic center indicated the
optimism of a thriving city.

Source: Proceedings of the Common Council of Milwaukee,
1924, Milwaukee, 1924, 2-3.

During the years since 1910 Milwaukee has achieved
the commanding leadership over all other American cities
in at least eighteen particulars. This is indeed a proud
record. It is for all of us to join in maintaining that
accomplishment and to add to these laurels as time pro-
ceeds. That they may be on record for our guidance, I
herewith enumerate some of the points in which our municipal government has assumed an undisputed leadership:

First: We are the only city bordering on a great inland waterway that has acquired ownership of the riparian
rights along that front.
Second: We are developing the greatest and best municipal harbor on the Great Lakes.
Third: We have constructed and are operating the finest and most economical street lighting system in this
country.
Fourth: We are given the credit of having the finest
and most up-to-date building code in America.
Fifth: The greatest authorities on city planning in
America have published broadly the fact that our city
planning activities are more studiously worked out and
further advanced than those of any other large American
city.
Sixth: No city can boast of such fine and beneficial
civic celebrations as held in Milwaukee. Among these are
the Sane Fourth, Community Christmas and Lake Front enter-
tainments.
Seventh: Our social center activities in our public
schools furnish clean recreation and excellent educational
instruction to great classes of our children and citizens
and are conceded to be the best in America.
Eighth: No city has a Continuation School the equal
of ours either in character of the building or in the num-

ber of courses provided. This structure moreover, was
paid for largely in cash instead of bonds.

Ninth: The Sewerage System is one of the finest in
the world. More than $4,000,000 of the cost of this has
been paid for in cash instead of bonds. This system will
be in actual operation in about one year and we hope it
will do much to improve our water supply.

Tenth: We are the first and only government to place
the purchase of lands for city purchases upon a real
business basis. No other city has an experienced real
estate agent to conduct this work at a tremendous saving
in money.

Eleventh: No other city has so little unemployment
as Milwaukee. This is particularly true during times of
industrial depression. Our diversified industry, together with the fine co-operative spirit shown by our unemployment committees, as well as our governmental employment bureau has tended to relieve this problem.

Twelfth: No other city has undertaken to solve the
housing problem as has Milwaukee. With the co-operation
of our city and county governments together with public
spirited citizens, we have shown other American cities
how it is possible to construct homes, modest but modern,
for working people at a saving of $1,500 each.

Thirteen: No other city has the low crime record of
Milwaukee. There was, for instance, only one murder per
100,000 population in this city during the last year,
where there was an average of 9 per 100,000 population in
every other large American city.

Fourteen: No other city can boast of so fine a police, fire or water departments as has our city.

Fifteenth: While no other city can boast of more
public improvements, still our per capita bonded debt is
the lowest of thirty-five of the largest cities in this
country.

Sixteenth: According to the greatest authority on the
subject in this nation, Judge Charles B. Wood of Chicago,
we gave the best financial credit of any American city.

Seventeenth: Better than this, we are the only city
that has made provision to wipe out our public debt entirely: by the establishment of an amortization fund and
by the enactment of a statute making it mandatory for the
city to add to this fund each year, the monies set aside
will accumulate interest and compound interest until within forty years we can acclaim to the world that we have
wiped out our entire public debt and thereby hand down to
the future, the hope and possibility of greatly reduced
taxation.

Eighteenth: No other large city has so little labor
trouble. There are fewer strikes here and less disorder,
when one occurs, than in any other large city. This has
been achieved, on the one hand, by an intelligent and
wholesome recognition of the limitations of the present

wage system, and on the other hand, by a fulfillment of
our duty to assist the workers in every struggle for a
better man and womanhood and a higher civilization.

In view of these, and other accomplishments, Milwaukee is recognized today by students of government as
the leader among American cities. We think in terms of
progress, not reaction. Our patriotism is that of love,
not of hatred. Our spirit is that of homes, not of dives.
Out ethics is of respect for all peoples and their reli-
gions. Our Americanism is that of right, tolerance, liberty and justice as written in the Declaration of Independence, Bill of Rights and the life of Abraham Lincoln.

Milwaukee, in short, is the first large city in
America that has started to apply successfully, the ab-
stract principle of Americanism in the concrete realm of
equal opportunities for the people.

HOAN MEETS THE CHALLENGE OF THE DEPRESSION
1936

Even after the state legislature
defeated the consolidation proposals, Mayor Hoan still asserted
that "no other city in the world
has accomplished so much in gen-
uine governmental improvement in
so short a period of time." His
innovative approach to city affairs was again illustrated during the Great Depression, when
he introduced the use of scrip
issued by the city of Milwaukee
that alleviated the suffering
of public employees.

Source: Daniel W. Hoan, <u>City Government. The Record of
the Milwaukee Experiment</u>, New York: Harcourt, Brace &
Co., 1936, 164-173.

My first thought was that a solution lay in the issuance of some sort of municipal currency. The municipal
credit was of the very best. If we were short of cash,
we held in lieu thereof for every dollar of unpaid taxes,
a tax certificate. After three successive defaults and
the consequent issuance of three tax certificates on any
piece of real estate, the city could take title and become the sole owner of that property clear and free of all
encumbrances. In other words, if every taxpayer should
finally default on his taxes, the local government would
automatically become the sole proprietor of all the property within the city limits for about 10 per cent of its
real value. What better security could there be, as any
municipal currency issued would be promptly redeemed either in payment of taxes or cash coming from rents or the
re-sale of any property the city must acquire?

The sole difficulty was whether or not the cooperation of business houses could be obtained in the acceptance of the currency or scrip in ordinary business transactions. In other words, did the people of Milwaukee
have faith in themselves?

To sound out sentiment, I sent to the Common Council
in December, 1932, a communication advocating the issuance of a sufficient amount of municipal currency or scrip
to enable the meeting of all payrolls or bills with 75
per cent in Federal currency and 25 in local money, called
scrip. This money had the advantage of bearing no interest and would save the city over one hundred thousand
dollars annually. It had the disadvantage of being re-

deemable once a year, as it would be received in payment
of taxes and destroyed when thus returned. If circulated
readily in business, it would increase transactions by
millions of dollars.

The test was on. Newspapers opened fire. Public
hearings were held. The officers of banks and representatives of the Real Estate Board, the Association of Commerce, taxpayers' leagues, and what not all denounced the
plan as sheer folly. In one chorus they demanded that
the budget be cut down to meet the actual cash received.
It did not seem to matter if health work was crippled;
if schools were run on half time; if streets were un-
lighted; if playgrounds shut down. No matter what happened, the budget must be cut and hundreds of city laborers turned out on the streets to beg for relief, inci-
dentally thus increasing the tax burden. Inadvertently,
at the time one of the bank representatives admitted that
if this currency were to draw interest it would not be
so bad.

The result of all this onslaught was that the Common
Council by a narrow margin defeated the plan. Not to be
worsted, I took up the banker's remark and said, "Well,
if we must pay interest, we will issue an iron-clad baby
bond redeemable at the end of four years and drawing a
5 per cent interest charge." This alteration in plan was
enough to secure the needed votes. Big business had won
its interest concession, but the city itself was to make
the greatest gain. . . .

The bonds were engraved on specially made and designed paper to prevent counterfeiting. They were issued
in denominations of one, five, ten, and one hundred dollars. The ones and fives drew no interest. They were
used for the sake of convenience in making immediate payments and were exchangeable for the ten and one hundred
dollar interest-bearing bonds.

While the bonds were issued for four years, they
could be used in the meantime in payment of any delinquent
tax bill. For convenience' sake, four interest coupons
were attached to each bond, each good for a year's interest when due on the particular bond. Thus, the holder
had only to clip the coupon as with an ordinary bond, de-
liver it to the city at the end of the given year, and
secure his cash. The device greatly simplified the municipal bookkeeping.

The city was now ready to issue its own money, scrip.
bonds, notes, or whatever you might wish to call it. We
decided to pay half of each payroll in ordinary cash and
half in municipal money. How were we to fare in its acceptance by merchants, banks, and so on? We had every
suspicion--which subsequently proved true--that no bank
would honor this currency. They flatly and curtly turned
their thumbs down. We visited the big department stores
to enlist their cooperation. Their answer was a decided

negative.   Next in line came the privately owned public
utilities, gas, electric, and telephone. Would they accept this impudent scrip? Decidedly not! This general
attitude, though not unexcepted, was a serious jar.

We assembled the city department heads, and informed
them of the nature and importance of the fight.   They
must make every single city employee realize that the
disposal of this currency at less than par value was an
injury to every other employee; that each department must
form a distress committee to help out with cash or advice
any distressed member. This worked admirably.   The employees eventually won the fight.   The smaller merchants,
through their organizations, were made thoroughly acquainted with the soundness of the currency.   They were
quick to see that since the larger stores would not receive it, the total sales of the smaller units would be
nicely enhanced if they honored the local money. All who
lined up were placed on an honor list, which was circulated among city employees who quickly switched their patronage to these friendly merchants. . . .

Thus passed a vital incident in the city's history.
What had been gained? What had been lost?

The city unearthed a brand new means of borrowing
money, or rather an escape from bank-borrowing, through
the issuance of its own money. The municipality was
forced into the banking business for this purpose and the
sale of its own gilt-edge bonds over its own counter.
The city by its new device built up an unshakeable credit
among its own common citizenry, and freed itself for all
time from being obliged to borrow from banks or bankers.
Thus there was no further danger of bank dictation in
municipal affairs. . . .

Thus Milwaukee's municipal currency experiment improved the city's financial standing all along the line.
Due credit for the experience must be given to both the
depression and our friends of the banking fraternity.

NEGRO PROTEST IN MILWAUKEE
1963

Like many American cities, Milwaukee only reluctantly accomo-
dated itself to the Civil Rights
Revolution of the 1960s. Its
growing black population was bit-
ter and frustrated by the city's
inability to secure for them e-
qual rights on the job, in housing or in the schools. In a public statement, leaders of the
black community criticized Mayor
Henry Maier and demanded reforms.

Source: The Milwaukee Journal, July 25, 1963.

We, the undersigned citizens, interested in establishing the kind of community where every individual may
develop his full potential, are gravely concerned with
the apparent negative reaction of official Milwaukee to
the present rightful demands of this country's Negro population. The fact that these demands are in keeping with
democratic principles is too elementary and fundamental
for extended argument. In the present world-wide struggle
for individual freedom, America cannot afford to waver
in its commitment to democratic ideals lest the very
foundations of freedom are endangered.

President John F. Kennedy, in his recent nation-
wide address on civil rights, challenged all Americans to
totally commit themselves to the realization of equal
opportunity for all, regardless of race, religion, or national origin. The president thus set the moral tone for
dealing with this crucial question, and committed himself
and his administration to achieving this goal, the legal
basis of which no longer can be doubted. Mr. Kennedy
asked state and local leaders to fulfill their responsibilities in reaching a peaceful and immediate solution
to this problem.

In view of these developments, it is disappointing
that the mayor of our city, by his words and actions, has
beclouded the hopes and aspirations of Milwaukee Negroes
and the entire city of Milwaukee in achieving the goals
so ably outlined by the president. Of course, this lack
of concern with racial problems has been all too sadly
apparent long before now.

Milwaukee has racial problems of a most serious nature. Attention must be given to these immediately if
Milwaukee is to enjoy an orderly adjustment to social
changes which are inevitable.

Fair housing policies are desperately needed in the city of Milwaukee. It is not enough to say that this is a problem of statewide concern -- it is a problem which must be dealt with at both state and local levels. Legalisms and jurisdictional issues must give way to the realization of legislation designed to aid in the achievement of equal opportunity for good housing.

Employment opportunities for Negroes, both in the skilled and unskilled categories, are grossly inadequate. Unions have failed to provide adequate opportunities for apprenticeship training, and industry has not generally accepted Negroes in "on the job" training programs. Equal opportunity for decent jobs can instill human dignity and responsibility. Segregated neighborhoods in Milwaukee have resulted in de facto segregation of schools and recreational facilities. These need immediate attention.

In addition, we note the meager involvement and participation of Negroes in the operations of city government. Presently, too few Negroes serve on appointed policy making boards and commissions. Five Negroes are members of the Milwaukee Commission on Community Relations, which is only advisory and not policy making. We are keenly aware that political considerations are inevitably involved in the selection of such appointees. However, leadership in a democracy must consider incentive or motivational implications for involving, in a substantial way, the Negro segment of the community in running the affairs of the community. This is a must for self-government and an important consideration for the maintenance of a stable democratic society.

These problems are so closely interrelated that they must be attacked on all fronts in order to make meaningful achievements in any one area. These problems must be faced; they will not solve themselves. These problems must be dealt with in a constructive and progressive manner.

In this effort, the leadership of the mayor's office, despite its legal limitations, is imperative and essential. Could not the mayor, for example, following the leadership of President Kennedy, begin to use all the powers at his command -- legal, persuasive, ceremonial and otherwise -- to foster the kind of communication and co-operation between white and Negro leaders in these various areas? Could he not see that city hall policies, by his own example, influence that which community leaders do? Could not the mayor and common council provide moral leadership in the present crisis?

It is praiseworthy that the press (e.g., several editorials have appeared in The Milwaukee Journal and the Milwaukee Star), an important public opinion shaper with corresponding important responsibilities, has expressed its concern that city hall should assert more leadership

in facing racial problems. As praiseworthy as this is,
however, only the mayor has the overall vantage point,
power and prestige to rally the kind of forces necessary,
including the press, to cope with these problems.

The present mayor is in a position to make enduring
the positive contributions in race relations. Whether
he takes immediate action now can have an impact on all
Milwaukee for many years to come, or he can remain com-
placent and allow the racial situation to worsen as it
has in other communities.

As President Kennedy stated in his nation-wide address on civil rights, "Those who do nothing are inviting
shame as well as violence. Those who act boldly are recognizing right as well as reality."

We call upon labor, business, the press, civic
groups and churches to encourage the mayor to assume the
responsibilities of leadership in this area of race relations. We call upon the common council to give leadership in this area also.

In a democracy, leaders sometimes have to deal with
problems that might not be politically popular or expedient, but the solutions to which can bring about more
enduring democratic foundations.

MAYOR HENRY MAIER PREACHES THE "MILWAUKEE IDEA"
1964

> If Maier was at first unrespon-
> sive to the demands of the black
> community, it was perhaps because
> of his preoccupation with issues
> that threatened Milwaukee's very
> survival. An "iron ring" of se-
> gregated suburbs surrounded the
> city, enclaves created to keep
> core problems from their door-
> steps. Industrial obsolescence
> and budgetary restrictions posed
> long term dangers to the city
> economy. Maier's second inaug-
> ural address on April 21, 1964,
> urged implementation of what he
> labeled "The Milwaukee Idea."

Source: Proceedings of the Common Council of the City of
Milwaukee, Milwaukee, 1964, 2-7.

During the past four years, in keeping with the Milwaukee Idea, we have succeeded in setting up programs and
organizations to deal with the basic social, economic,
and physical problems of the community.

During the past four years, the Milwaukee Idea has
enlisted the talents and support of labor, business, the
professions, and the universities to work towards the
solution of our problems.

The Milwaukee Idea now calls for a greater understanding of our problems and renewed efforts on the part
of all to produce solutions.

Above all, the Milwaukee Idea now calls for a
broader recognition of the crucial problem of mustering
the resources we must have in order to meet our problems.

It calls for a recognition by all those who make demands on our resources, that they must also help us find
ways to replenish those resources.

It's time they not only point out what Milwaukee
should do, but also recognize what Milwaukee can do within its presently limited resources.

While the City of Milwaukee will continue to meet
its responsibilities, we can no longer afford the game of
let's pretend:

The suburban pretense that we can shoulder all the
burdens laid upon us without adequate compensation--and
this includes the weighted costs to us of the expressway
system and the disproportionate weight of tax-exempt property of service to the entire area;

The local critics' pretense that we can do every-
thing at once, without insisting on priorities of action;
The metropolitan pretense that we can meet our prob-
lems--the great problems of urban growth and change--
without also taking steps to enlarge our resources.
If our tax rate is rising, if, as is forseeable, our
resources cannot meet our expenditures, what do we do?
Do we cut back or eliminate our services?
Do we add new taxes?
Do we increase our already heavy debt load?
Or do we retain our level of services, stabilize our
debt, add no new taxes by:
First, working for greater economy and efficiency
in government;
Second, by correcting inequities that now exist between Milwaukee and other units of government;
And finally, and very importantly, by developing our
own economic and human resources.
This latter three-fold course is my recommendation.
. . .
During the next four years the Milwaukee Idea faces
one of its severest challenges in the fight for economic
development. The high geared race for industry compels
us to run very, very fast just to keep even--let alone
surge ahead.
If you doubt the danger, just think of the many
aging plants we have. What will happen when they reach
the point of obsolescence? Will ne plants be built here
or will the entire operation be relocated to the low tax-
low wage areas of the South? What about the threat of
industrial bond financing, which is costing us one Cutler-
Hammer plant? How many such enticements will we encounter
in the future?
As I see it, our top priority in the next four years
is to go on a "war footing" in the nation-wide battle for
plants. We must step up our defenses to stop or at least
reduce the pillaging of our existing industries and, at
the same time, begin mounting a strong counter-offensive
aimed at capturing some new plants ourselves. . . .
And while discussing economic development, we must
recognize that it embraces more than just industrial development. I particularly call your attention to the
carefully drawn proposal for a Milwaukee world festival.
The decision as to whether such a festival is feasi-
ble rests primarily with the private sector of the economy. The decision should be made soon.
But the festival, if it is found financially feasi-
ble, should be viewed from more than a money-making stand-
point. There is little doubt that Milwaukee does not receive as much national and international attention as it
deserves, principally because very few outsiders know anything about us. The festival would be one way of telling
the Milwaukee story to the world.

It is certainly in accord with the Milwaukee Idea
of preserving the best of our traditions even as we go
forward in the modern world.

This is certainly a concern of the larger Milwaukee
community--not just the City of Milwaukee alone.

Again, when we speak of the problem of equal opportunities for minorities we are talking about more than a
City of Milwaukee problem. At the moment this is our
nation's number one piece of unfinished business.

The city government is moving to meet its responsibilities in this complex area, but there will be no solution until people wake to the fact that for Milwaukee
this is a metropolitan problem requiring the full moral
and economic resources of the metropolitan community.
. . .

We have done and are doing much more than this, but
all these efforts will be ineffective so long as the metropolitan area outside of the City of Milwaukee fails
to recognize the fact that one of the greatest causes
of minority segregation is the segregation that exists
between the central city and the suburbs.

Until full recognition is made of this fact, we
live in a world made safe for hypocrisy. It is nothing
less than hypocrisy for those outside the city to call on
the people of this city and especially the economically
insecure to undertake the entire burden of this crucial
social adjustment, when it is only in the city that you
can actually find peoples of different races, creeds,
and economic levels living together, working together,
and worshipping together to any significant degree.

It is time to end this hypocricy, and it is time for
a wider recognition of the responsibilities of everyone
in the metropolitan area towards meeting the complex
problems of social change. . . .

MAYOR MAIER DESCRIBES AMERICA'S URBAN CRISIS
1972

Today Milwaukee suffers, as do all
American cities, under the crushing weight of a shrinking tax base,
racial unrest, and a lack of national effort. Mayor Maier, who
was first to demand a "reordering"
of national priorities, has become
a leading spokesman not only for
Wisconsin's cities but also for
the national urban community. In
his presidential address to the
U. S. Conference of Mayors (June
17, 1972) he demanded aid to lo-
calities through the State and
Local Fiscal Assistance Act and
assessed the national urban condition.

Source: City Problems of 1972. Proceedings of the Forti-
eth Annual Conference, United States Conference of Mayors,
Washington, 1972, 9-10.

The Congress must recognize that local fiscal assistance is one of the most pressing needs of the nation,
and at least on a par with all other spending requirements
of America. . . .
A decade ago, when the voices of America's Mayors
tried to catch the ears of our national leaders in Congress and the Executive Branch, we were voices crying in
the wilderness. In that decade we warned them, and much
has happened to bear out our grim prophecies. Problems
which had been swept under the rug of national indifference and into the dark corners of urban neglect have been
illuminated by the frightening infernos which have swept
through some of our major cities, leaving twisted rubble
in their wake.
I think we are finally beginning to impress upon our
national leaders that when the Mayors speak, they are
speaking not on their own behalf, but they are expressing
the inarticulated demands of the restless majority who
want the national debate over policies and priorities to
come to grips with the real problems that they face in
places where they live in America.
We speak for the tormented taxpayer groaning under
the crushing burden of local property taxes he must bear,
a tax which was never intended to solve the nation's domestic ills.
We speak for the bewildered inner city resident who

reads that Congress has appropriated billions for housing
and neighborhood renewal, but who finds that these billions somehow never seem to break through the bureaucra-
tic barriers erected by federal officials so that decent
housing can be built where it is most needed.

And we speak for all of the frustrated citizens of
America's cities who want their cities to be capable of
coping with the pressing problems which beset them.

And, although this may sound surprising to some, we
speak for the harried satellite cities of the central
cities, if not for the gold coast suburbs. The view from
the picture window has changed. The tough, stubborn problems central cities have grappled with for decades are
now appearing at the other end of the freeway.

In this, as in any accounting of stewardship, there
are things which happened in the past year towards which
we can count as pulses and say "Mission Accomplished";
there are others that certainly remain in the category
of unfinished business.

We were successful in securing 150,000 public service
jobs - not enough, but no small achievement in the face of
a previous Presidential veto. But again, here we are at
the end of the school term not knowing how much of a summer youth program we will have to work with.

In spite of Congressional indifference and executive
surrender, we were able to keep urban renewal alive.

We gained acceptance of the principle that mass transit programs cannot work without mass subsidies, but the
Federal-Aid Highway and Mass Transportation Act remains
unenacted. . . .

We need the full $500 million authorized to honor
the letters of intent that cities have sent to HUD to
apply for open space land program grants.

We need funding at the authorized level of $1.75
billion for law enforcement assistance programs, and a re-
direction of the Safe Streets Act program so that the
money is spent in the streets of the cities and not the
rural lanes of our villages.

We need a federal takeover and reform of the welfare
system; full funding of the authorized $6 billion for
elementary and secondary schools; and enactment of a national health insurance plan, more hospitals, neighborhood health centers, intermediate care centers, and mo-
dernization of outmoded hospital facilities, and a Special Action Office for Drug Abuse.

And finally, we need an understanding of the fact
that what we are talking about is not programs, but people. Not unemployment programs, but the man without a
job and a family to support. Not housing programs, but
families forced to live in horribly run-down rat-traps.
Not drug abuse programs, but young lives burned out by
drugs before they get a chance to live. Not crime prevention programs, but fearful older citizens afraid to

walk their neighborhood streets. Not anti-pollution
programs, but people whose lives are shortened by the
poisoned air they breathe and the water they drink; and,
yes, waters in which children will never learn to fish.

The programs are only a means. The welfare of the
people is our end concern.

BIBLIOGRAPHY

Milwaukee, like any other modern American city, produces each year a prodigious amount of official documents that describe its functioning. These Annual Reports, from the Annuity Commission through the Zoning Board, are of vast interest to those seeking specific information, but are almost incomprehensible to the layman and of little concern to him. The purpose of this bibliography is not to list Reports that are of minimal interest, but rather to present a full listing of secondary work on the growth and development of the city of Milwaukee. The majority of the works listed will be found in any good reference library. Readers who seek further information as to specific aspects of Milwaukee's life would do well to begin with the brief yet extremely informative Annual Directory and Report of Milwaukee's Progress. In the Milwaukee City Hall an extremely efficient Legislative Reference Bureau stands ready to aid the interested citizen or the demanding scholar.

Anderson, William J. and Bleyer, Julius (eds). Milwaukee's Great Industries. Milwaukee, 1892.

As the Journal Told It. Selections from Past Issues of the Milwaukee Journal. Milwaukee, 1945.

Aukofer, Frank A. City with a Chance. Milwaukee, 1968. Analysis of the July 1967 riots that deals with causes, effects, the failures of Henry Maier and expectations for the future.

Austin, H. Russell. The Milwaukee Story: The Making of an American City. Milwaukee, 1946. A Journal reporter who put together a short, popular yet professional history in honor of the Centennial celebrations.

Banyai, A. L. and Beleznay, Frank. The Hungarians of the City of Milwaukee. Milwaukee, 1929.

Barton, E. E. Industrial History of Milwaukee. Milwaukee, 1886.

Blied, Benjamin. Three Archbishops of Milwaukee. Milwaukee, 1955.

Borum, Thaddeus. We, the Milwaukee Poles. Milwaukee, 1946.

Braun, Berton G. The Milwaukee Police Department.
     Analysis of the most successful police forces in the
     nation, one famed for its toughness and its honesty.

Bridges to the Future. A Capital Improvement Program for
     the City of Milwaukee, 1954 through 1959. Milwau-
     kee, 1954.

Bruce, William George. Builders of Milwaukee. Milwau-
     kee, 1946.

--------------------. I Was Born in America. Milwau-
     kee, 1937. The autobiography of a man who was a
     local historian, harbor consultant and city booster.

--------------------. Short History of Milwaukee, Wis-
     consin. Milwaukee, 1936.

--------------------. The Auditorium. Milwaukee, 1909.

--------------------. (ed.) History of Milwaukee. City
     and County. 3 v. Chicago, 1922.

Buck, James S. Pioneer History of Milwaukee. 4 v. Mil-
     waukee, 1876-1886. Probably the best of the early
     chronicles of city development.

Campbell, Henry C. et. al. Wisconsin in Three Centuries.
     4 v. New York, 1906.

Chapman, Silas. Hand Book of Wisconsin. Milwaukee, 1855.
     An immigrant's guide that claimed Milwaukee was
     greater than Chicago.

Charter of the City of Milwaukee and Ordinances in Force,
     May 22, 1848. Milwaukee, 1848.

Charter Ordinances of the City of Milwaukee, containing
     all the charter ordinances passed by the common coun-
     cil. . . through November 25, 1946. Milwaukee, 1946.

Citizen's Bureau of Milwaukee. Financial Survey of the
     Local Governments. . . for the Ten Years 1922 to
     1931 Inclusive. Milwaukee, 1932.

Cochran, Thomas Childs. The Pabst Brewing Company: The
     History of an American Business. New York, 1948.
     A model business history of an extraordinary company.

Colver, James Newton (ed.). One Hundred Years of Metho-
     dism in Greater Milwaukee. Milwaukee, 1935.

Commons, John. Eighteen Months' Work. Milwaukee, 1912.

Report on efforts to rationalize the Milwaukee government that Commons carried out for Socialist Mayor
Seidel.

Conrad, Howard Lewis. History of Milwaukee from Its Settlement to the Year 1895, 2 v. Chicago, 1895.

Cronau, Rudolph. Prohibition and the Destruction of the
American Brewing Industry. New York, 1926.

Davis, Richard S. 50 Years of Architecture. Milwaukee,
1943. Analysis of the buildings done by the Esch-
weller family of architects.

----------------. "Milwaukee, Old Lady Thrift" in Robert
S. Allen (ed.). Our Fair City. New York, 1947.

Derby, William Edward. A History of the Port of Milwaukee. Madison, 1963.

Derleth, August William. The Milwaukee Road, Its First
Hundred Years. New York, 1948. A history of the
corporate trials of the railroad, with emphasis on
the role of Alexander Mitchell.

Desmond, Humphrey J. "Early Irish Settlers in Milwaukee,"
Wisconsin Magazine of History, XIII (1930).

Deutsch, Herman J. "Yankee and Teuton Rivalry in Wisconsin Politics of the Seventies," Wisconsin Magazine
of History, XIV (1930-31).

Early Milwaukee. Milwaukee, 1916. An edition of papers
and reminiscences compiled by the Old Settlers Club.

Evening Wisconsin Newspaper Reference Book. Milwaukee,
1914.

Everest, Kate. "How Wisconsin Came by its large German
Element," Collections of the State Historical Society of Wisconsin, XII (1892).

Filtzer, Robert and Slayton, William L. Manufacturing
in Milwaukee and 22 Metropolitan Cities, 1919, 1929,
1939. Milwaukee, 1944.

Final Report of the Mayor's Study Group on Social Problems in the Inner Core Area. Milwaukee, 1960.

Flower, Frank A. History of Milwaukee, Wisconsin. Chicago, 1881.

Frank, Louis Frederick. The Medical History of Milwaukee,

_1834-1914_. Milwaukee, 1915.

General Ordinances of the City of Milwaukee up to January
     1, 1896. Milwaukee, 1896.

Givens, Richard A., "The Milwaukee Brewery Strike of
     1953," University of Wisconsin M. A. thesis, 1954.

Glassberg, Benjamin. Across the Desk of a Relief Adminis-
     trator. Chicago, 1938. An account of the difficul-
     ties of administering out-door relief in Milwaukee
     during the Depression.

Goff, Charles D. "The Politics of Governmental Integra-
     tion in Metropolitan Milwaukee," 2 v., Northwestern
     University Ph.D. dissertation, 1952.

Gregory, John Goadby. History of Milwaukee, Wisconsin,
     3 v. Chicago, 1931.

--------------------. (ed.). Southeastern Wisconsin. A
     History of Old Milwaukee County, 4 v. Chicago, 1932.
     The first volume concerns itself almost exclusively
     with the history of Milwaukee.

Hamming, Edward. The Port of Milwaukee. Chicago, 1952.

Hanson, Bertil. A Report on the Politics of Milwaukee.
     Cambridge, 1961.

Harding, Henry M. General Engineering Report to the Har-
     bor Commission of the City of Milwaukee, Wisconsin.
     Milwaukee, 1920. A crucial document that used busi-
     ness information as well as technical expertise to
     plan development of the next quarter century.

Harger, Charles. Milwaukee Illustrated: Its Trade, Com-
     merce, Manufacturing Interests and Advantages as a
     Residence City. Milwaukee, 1877.

Haynes, Rowland. A Recreation Survey. Milwaukee, 1912.

---------------. How Much Playground Space Does a City
     Need? Milwaukee, 1917.

Hillquit, Morris. History of Socialism in the United
     States. New York, 1906.

History of Brewing and the Growth of the United States
     Brewers' Association. New York, 1937.

History of Milwaukee, Wisconsin. Chicago, 1881. This
     vast 1800-page history by the Western Historical

Company includes almost 4,000 biographical sketches.

History of the Milwaukee Social-Democratic Victories.
    Milwaukee, 1911.

Hoan, Daniel. _City Government. The Record of the Milwau-
    kee Experiment_. New York, 1936.

----------- . (comp.). _Charter of the City of Milwaukee
    . . . including the Laws of 1913_. Milwaukee, 1914.

Hooker, William Francis. _Bill Hooker's Old-Time Milwau-
    kee and Men Who Helped Make it Great_. Milwaukee,
    1935.

----------------------. _Glimpses of an Earlier Milwau-
    kee_. Milwaukee, 1929. Both volumes are reminis-
    censes of the 1880-1910 period by a former _Journal_
    reporter who also managed Mayor Becker's election in
    1906.

Howard, William W. "The City of Milwaukee," _Harper's
    Weekly_, 35 (July, 1891).

Howe, Frederick C. "Milwaukee, a Socialist City," _The
    Outlook_, 95 (June, 1910).

Johnson, F. H. _Brief Record of the Development of the
    Milwaukee Road_. Chicago, 1939.

Johnson, Peter Leo. "Milwaukee's First Mass," _Wisconsin
    Magazine of History_, XXVII (1943). Summarizes the
    arguments and concludes it occurred in August, 1835.

Kellogg, Louise Phelps. "The Beginnings of Milwaukee,"
    Wisconsin Magazine of History, I (June, 1917).

----------------------. "The Bennett Law in Wisconsin,"
    Wisconsin Magazine of History, II (September, 1918).

Kerstein, Edward S. _Milwaukee's All-American Mayor.
    Portrait of Daniel Webster Hoan_. Englewood Cliffs,
    New Jersey, 1966.

Kilbourn, Bryon. _Review of the Report Made by the Com-
    mittee of Investigation. . . Relating to the Land
    Grant_. Milwaukee, 1858. A spirited defense against
    the bribery scandal that ultimately forced him into
    Florida exile.

King, Charles. "The Cream City," _Cosmopolitan_, X (March,
    1891).

Korman, Gerd. <u>Industrialization, Immigrants and Americanizers; The View from Milwaukee, 1866-1921</u>. Madison, 1967.

Koss, Rudolph H. <u>Milwaukee</u>. Milwaukee, 1871. An excellent German language treatment of early city life.

Krieger, Elmer. <u>A Master Plan for the City of Milwaukee</u>. Milwaukee, 1947.

Kruger, Anne O. <u>The Impact of the St. Laurence Seaway on the Upper Midwest</u>. Minneapolis, 1963.

Kusik, Henry. <u>The Early Slovak Settlers of Milwaukee</u>. Milwaukee, 1930.

Lacher, John H. A. <u>The German Element in Wisconsin</u>. Milwaukee, 1925.

Lapham, Increase A. <u>Documentary History of the Milwaukee and Rock River Canal</u>. Milwaukee, 1840.

LaPiana, G. <u>The Italians in Milwaukee, Wisconsin</u>. Milwaukee, 1915.

Larson, Lawrence Marcellus. <u>A Financial and Administrative History of Milwaukee</u>. Madison, 1908. An accurate account which emphasizes the financial errors of early Milwaukee and how they were slowly rectified.

Legler, Henry E. <u>Leading Events of Wisconsin History</u>. Milwaukee, 1898.

Luening, Frederick W. <u>Land, Its Colonization -- The "Milwaukee Idea."</u> Milwaukee, 1919 (?) A proposed revitalization of Milwaukee through systematic land development by private corporations.

Lynaugh, Paula (comp.). <u>The Growth of Milwaukee's City Governmental Activities, 1846 to 1947, Inclusive</u>. Milwaukee, 1947.

MacArthur, Annabel Douglas. <u>Religion in Early Milwaukee</u>. Milwaukee, 1946.

Mack, Edwin S. "The Founding of Milwaukee," <u>Proceedings of the State Historical Society of Wisconsin</u>. 54 (1906).

MacKaya, Milton, "Milwaukee Gangless," New York, 1931. A condensed version of twelve articles that concluded the city was virtually free of organized crime.

Magyar, Francis. "History of the Early Milwaukee German
    Theatre," Wisconsin Magazine of History, XIII (1930).

Maier, Henry W. Challenge to the Cities. An Approach
    to a Theory of Urban Leadership. New York, 1966.
    A description of Maier's political science approach
    to decision making.

McDonald, Forrest. Let There Be Light: The Electric Uti-
    lity Industry in Wisconsin, 1881-1955. Madison,
    1957.

McMurtrie, Douglas C. Early Printing in Milwaukee. Mil-
    waukee, 1930.

Meisenheimer, L. G. "Milwaukee's Finances from One War
    to Another," Municipal Finance, XV (1943).

Merk, Frederick. Economic History of Wisconsin During
    the Civil War Decade. Madison, 1916.

Metropolitan Milwaukee. One Trade Area with 93 Local
    Governments. Milwaukee, 1936.

Milwaukee Harbor Project, "The Most Progressive Port on
    the Great Lakes." Milwaukee, 1936.

Milwaukee Illustrated. Milwaukee, 1910 (?). Probably
    the best picture history of turn of the century
    Milwaukee, with fascinating photographs of resort
    areas, homes and spas.

Milwaukee of Today. The Cream City of the Lakes. Mil-
    waukee, 1893.

Milwaukee. Seventy-five Years a City. Milwaukee, 1921.

Morrison, Andrew. The City of Milwaukee and State of Wis-
    consin. Milwaukee, 1888.

Mowry, Duane. "The Reign of Graft in Milwaukee," Arena,
    34 (December, 1905).

Municipal League of Milwaukee. Draft of an Act to Pre-
    vent Corrupt Practices in General and Primary Elec-
    tions. Milwaukee, 1896.

Nock, Albert Jay. "Socialism in Milwaukee," Outlook,
    CVII (1914).

Olin, Nelson. "Reminiscences of Milwaukee in 1835-36,"
    Wisconsin Magazine of History, XIII (1930).

One Hundred Years of Christian Service. Grand Avenue
    Congregational Church. Milwaukee, 1947.

"Pabst -- A Blue Ribbon Champion," Modern Brewery Age,
    26 (1941).

Preliminary Report on the Milwaukee River, July 1963.
    Milwaukee, 1963. A status report on the problems of
    cleaning up three polluted rivers, reopening public
    beaches, and fostering citizen concern with ecology.

Quaife, Milo. Wisconsin: Its History and Its People,
    4 v. Chicago, 1924.

Reinders, Robert. "Daniel W. Hoan and the Milwaukee So-
    cialist Party During the First World War," Wiscon-
    sin Magazine of History, XXXVI (1952).

Ruhland, George. Housing Conditions in Milwaukee. Mil-
    waukee, 1916.

Schenker, Eric. The Port of Milwaukee. Madison, 1967.
    A survey that makes an attempt to assess the impor-
    tance of the seaway.

Schlicher, J.J. "Hans Balatka and the Milwaukee Musical
    Society," Wisconsin Magazine of History, XXVII
    (1943), 40-55.

--------------. "The Milwaukee Musical Society in Time
    of Stress," Wisconsin Magazine of History, XXVII
    (1943), 178-93.

Schmandt, Henry J. The Milwaukee Metropolitan Study Com-
    mission. Bloomington, Indiana, 1965. The tragic
    story of an effort to rationalize Milwaukee area
    government which was balked by county and village
    ("iron ring") opposition.

Schmandt, Henry J., Golback, John C. and Vogel, Donald B.
    Milwaukee. A Contemporary Urban Profile. New York,
    1971.

Schulson, Florence. History of Planning Activity in Mil-
    waukee, 1892-1952. Milwaukee, 1952.

Sivyer, Charles M. Milwaukee's Babyhood. Milwaukee,
    1896.

Slayton, William L. (ed.). Blight Elimination and Urban
    Redevelopment in Milwaukee. Milwaukee, 1948.

Stearns, J. W. (ed.). The Columbia History of Education

in Wisconsin. New York, 1893. Patrick Donnelly's
chapter on Milwaukee is a useful summary.

Still, Bayard. Milwaukee. The History of a City. Madison, 1948. Written to coincied with Wisconsin's
Centennial, Still's colume remains the best scholar-
ly treatment; it is excellent on early land speculation.

-------------. "The Growth of Milwaukee as Recorded by
Contemporaries," Wisconsin Magazine of History, XXI
(1938).

-------------. "The Development of Milwaukee in the Early Metropolitan Period," Wisconsin Magazine of History, XXV (1942).

Tarantino, Thomas H. and Becker, Dismas (eds.). Welfare
Mothers Speak Out: We Ain't Gonna Shuffle Anymore.
New York, 1972.

The Lake Front in Milwaukee County. Milwaukee, 1940.

Thomann, Gallus. American Beer, Glimpses of its History
and Description of its Manufacture. New York, 1909.

Tien, H. Yuen (ed.). Milwaukee Metropolitan Area Fact
Book, 1940, 1950, and 1960. Madison, 1962. Statis-
tical analysis of the growth of the Milwaukee Stand-
ard Metropolitan Area.

Treleven, J. E. "The Milwaukee Bureau of Economy and
Efficiency," The Annals of the American Academy of
Political and Social Science, 41 (1912).

Wachman, Marvin. History of the Social-Democratic Party
of Milwaukee, 1897-1910. Urbana, Illinois, 1945.

Waring, George. Social Statistics of Cities. Washington, 1887. Analysis of the 1880 census with a historical survey of several American cities, including
Milwaukee.

Watrous, Jerome A. (ed.). Memoirs of Milwaukee County.
2 v. Madison, 1909.

Wells, Robert W. This is Milwaukee. New York, 1970. An
anecdotal and readable account; Milwaukee is a city
that grows slowly on its visitor, "like a beer
belly."

Werba, Arthur M. and Grunwald, John L. Making Milwaukee
Mightier. Milwaukee, 1929. A plea for governmental

consolidation which includes a detailed listing of
city annexations up to 1929.

Wheeler, Andrew Carpenter. The Chronicles of Milwaukee.
    Milwaukee, 1861. An account of early Milwaukee by
    one of its pioneers with a long section on the Bridge
    War.

Whitbeck, Ray H. The Geography and Economic Development
    of South-eastern Wisconsin. Madison, 1921.

Whyte, William F. "The Bennett Law Campaign," Wisconsin
    Magazine of History, X (1927).

Wolf, John Richardson. Wolf's Book of Milwaukee Dates;
    A Condensed History of Milwaukee. Milwaukee, 1915.

Zeidler, Frank. "The Expansion of the City of Milwaukee
    from 1940 to 1960," unpublished manuscript in the
    Milwaukee Public Library.

NAME INDEX